Henry VI, Part I by William Shakespeare

The life of William Shakespeare, arguably the most significant figure in the Western literary canon, is relatively unknown.

Shakespeare was born in Stratford-upon-Avon in 1565, possibly on the 23rd April, St. George's Day, and baptised there on 26th April.

Little is known of his education and the first firm facts to his life relate to his marriage, aged 18, to Anne Hathaway, who was 26 and from the nearby village of Shottery. Anne gave birth to their first son six months later.

Shakespeare's first play, The Comedy of Errors began a procession of real heavyweights that were to emanate from his pen in a career of just over twenty years in which 37 plays were written and his reputation forever established.

This early skill was recognised by many and by 1594 the Lord Chamberlain's Men were performing his works. With the advantage of Shakespeare's progressive writing they rapidly became London's leading company of players, affording him more exposure and, following the death of Queen Elizabeth in 1603, a royal patent by the new king, James I, at which point they changed their name to the King's Men.

By 1598, and despite efforts to pirate his work, Shakespeare's name was well known and had become a selling point in its own right on title pages.

No plays are attributed to Shakespeare after 1613, and the last few plays he wrote before this time were in collaboration with other writers, one of whom is likely to be John Fletcher who succeeded him as the house playwright for the King's Men.

William Shakespeare died two months later on April 23rd, 1616, survived by his wife, two daughters and a legacy of writing that none have since yet eclipsed.

Index of Contents

DRAMATIS PERSONAE

KING HENRY THE SIXTH.
DUKE OF GLOUCESTER, Uncle to the King, and Protector.
DUKE OF BEDFORD, Uncle to the King, Regent of France.
THOMAS BEAUFORT, Duke of Exeter, Great-uncle to the King.
HENRY BEAUFORT, Great-uncle to the King; Bishop of Winchester, and afterwards Cardinal.
JOHN BEAUFORT, Earl, afterwards Duke, of Somerset.
RICHARD PLANTAGENET, Son of Richard, late Earl of Cambridge; afterwards Duke of York.
EARL OF WARWICK.
EARL OF SALISBURY.
EARL OF SUFFOLK.
LORD TALBOT, afterwards Earl of Shrewsbury.
JOHN TALBOT, his Son.
EDMUND MORTIMER, Earl of March.
SIR JOHN FASTOLFE.
SIR WILLIAM LUCY.
SIR WILLIAM GLANSDALE.
SIR THOMAS GARGRAVE.
WOODVILE, Lieutenant of the Tower. Mayor of London. Mortimer's Keepers. A Lawyer.
VERNON, of the White-Rose, or York Faction.
BASSET, of the Red-Rose, or Lancaster Faction.
CHARLES, Dauphin, and afterwards King of France.
REIGNIER, Duke of Anjou, and titular King of Naples.
DUKE OF BURGUNDY.
DUKE OF ALENÇON.
BASTARD OF ORLEANS.

Governor of Paris.
Master-Gunner of Orleans, and his Son.
General of the French Forces in Bourdeaux.
A French Sergeant.
A Porter.
An old Shepherd, Father to Joan la Pucelle.

MARGARET, Daughter to Reignier; afterwards married to King Henry.
COUNTESS OF AUVERGNE.
JOAN LA PUCELLE, commonly called Joan of Arc.
Lords, Warders of the Tower, Heralds, Officers, Soldiers, Messengers, and Attendants.

Fiends appearing to La Pucelle.

SCENE.—Partly in England, and partly in France.

ACT I

SCENE I - Westminster Abbey

Dead March.

Enter the Funeral of KING HENRY the Fifth, attended on by Dukes of BEDFORD, Regent of France; GLOUCESTER, Protector; and EXETER, Earl of WARWICK, the BISHOP OF WINCHESTER, Heralds, & c

BEDFORD
Hung be the heavens with black, yield day to night!
Comets, importing change of times and states,
Brandish your crystal tresses in the sky,
And with them scourge the bad revolting stars
That have consented unto Henry's death!
King Henry the Fifth, too famous to live long!
England ne'er lost a king of so much worth.

GLOUCESTER
England ne'er had a king until his time.
Virtue he had, deserving to command:
His brandish'd sword did blind men with his beams:
His arms spread wider than a dragon's wings;
His sparking eyes, replete with wrathful fire,
More dazzled and drove back his enemies
Than mid-day sun fierce bent against their faces.
What should I say? his deeds exceed all speech:
He ne'er lift up his hand but conquered.

EXETER

We mourn in black: why mourn we not in blood?
Henry is dead and never shall revive:
Upon a wooden coffin we attend,
And death's dishonourable victory
We with our stately presence glorify,
Like captives bound to a triumphant car.
What! shall we curse the planets of mishap
That plotted thus our glory's overthrow?
Or shall we think the subtle-witted French
Conjurers and sorcerers, that afraid of him
By magic verses have contrived his end?

BISHOP OF WINCHESTER
He was a king bless'd of the King of kings.
Unto the French the dreadful judgement-day
So dreadful will not be as was his sight.
The battles of the Lord of hosts he fought:
The church's prayers made him so prosperous.

GLOUCESTER
The church! where is it? Had not churchmen pray'd,
His thread of life had not so soon decay'd:
None do you like but an effeminate prince,
Whom, like a school-boy, you may over-awe.

BISHOP OF WINCHESTER
Gloucester, whate'er we like, thou art protector
And lookest to command the prince and realm.
Thy wife is proud; she holdeth thee in awe,
More than God or religious churchmen may.

GLOUCESTER
Name not religion, for thou lovest the flesh,
And ne'er throughout the year to church thou go'st
Except it be to pray against thy foes.

BEDFORD
Cease, cease these jars and rest your minds in peace:
Let's to the altar: heralds, wait on us:
Instead of gold, we'll offer up our arms:
Since arms avail not now that Henry's dead.
Posterity, await for wretched years,
When at their mothers' moist eyes babes shall suck,
Our isle be made a nourish of salt tears,
And none but women left to wail the dead.
Henry the Fifth, thy ghost I invocate:
Prosper this realm, keep it from civil broils,
Combat with adverse planets in the heavens!
A far more glorious star thy soul will make
Than Julius Caesar or bright--

Enter a MESSENGER

MESSENGER
My honourable lords, health to you all!
Sad tidings bring I to you out of France,
Of loss, of slaughter and discomfiture:
Guienne, Champagne, Rheims, Orleans,
Paris, Guysors, Poictiers, are all quite lost.

BEDFORD
What say'st thou, man, before dead Henry's corse?
Speak softly, or the loss of those great towns
Will make him burst his lead and rise from death.

GLOUCESTER
Is Paris lost? is Rouen yielded up?
If Henry were recall'd to life again,
These news would cause him once more yield the ghost.

EXETER
How were they lost? what treachery was used?

MESSENGER
No treachery; but want of men and money.
Amongst the soldiers this is muttered,
That here you maintain several factions,
And whilst a field should be dispatch'd and fought,
You are disputing of your generals:
One would have lingering wars with little cost;
Another would fly swift, but wanteth wings;
A third thinks, without expense at all,
By guileful fair words peace may be obtain'd.
Awake, awake, English nobility!
Let not sloth dim your horrors new-begot:
Cropp'd are the flower-de-luces in your arms;
Of England's coat one half is cut away.

EXETER
Were our tears wanting to this funeral,
These tidings would call forth their flowing tides.

BEDFORD
Me they concern; Regent I am of France.
Give me my steeled coat. I'll fight for France.
Away with these disgraceful wailing robes!
Wounds will I lend the French instead of eyes,
To weep their intermissive miseries.

Enter to them another MESSENGER

MESSENGER

Lords, view these letters full of bad mischance.
France is revolted from the English quite,
Except some petty towns of no import:
The Dauphin Charles is crowned king of Rheims;
The Bastard of Orleans with him is join'd;
Reignier, Duke of Anjou, doth take his part;
The Duke of Alencon flieth to his side.

EXETER
The Dauphin crowned king! all fly to him!
O, whither shall we fly from this reproach?

GLOUCESTER
We will not fly, but to our enemies' throats.
Bedford, if thou be slack, I'll fight it out.

BEDFORD
Gloucester, why doubt'st thou of my forwardness?
An army have I muster'd in my thoughts,
Wherewith already France is overrun.

Enter another MESSENGER

MESSENGER
My gracious lords, to add to your laments,
Wherewith you now bedew King Henry's hearse,
I must inform you of a dismal fight
Betwixt the stout Lord Talbot and the French.

BISHOP OF WINCHESTER
What! wherein Talbot overcame? is't so?

MESSENGER
O, no; wherein Lord Talbot was o'erthrown:
The circumstance I'll tell you more at large.
The tenth of August last this dreadful lord,
Retiring from the siege of Orleans,
Having full scarce six thousand in his troop.
By three and twenty thousand of the French
Was round encompassed and set upon.
No leisure had he to enrank his men;
He wanted pikes to set before his archers;
Instead whereof sharp stakes pluck'd out of hedges
They pitched in the ground confusedly,
To keep the horsemen off from breaking in.
More than three hours the fight continued;
Where valiant Talbot above human thought
Enacted wonders with his sword and lance:
Hundreds he sent to hell, and none durst stand him;
Here, there, and every where, enraged he flew:
The French exclaim'd, the devil was in arms;

All the whole army stood agazed on him:
His soldiers spying his undaunted spirit
A Talbot! a Talbot! cried out amain
And rush'd into the bowels of the battle.
Here had the conquest fully been seal'd up,
If Sir John Fastolfe had not play'd the coward:
He, being in the vaward, placed behind
With purpose to relieve and follow them,
Cowardly fled, not having struck one stroke.
Hence grew the general wreck and massacre;
Enclosed were they with their enemies:
A base Walloon, to win the Dauphin's grace,
Thrust Talbot with a spear into the back,
Whom all France with their chief assembled strength
Durst not presume to look once in the face.

BEDFORD

Is Talbot slain? then I will slay myself,
For living idly here in pomp and ease,
Whilst such a worthy leader, wanting aid,
Unto his dastard foemen is betray'd.

MESSENGER

O no, he lives; but is took prisoner,
And Lord Scales with him and Lord Hungerford:
Most of the rest slaughter'd or took likewise.

BEDFORD

His ransom there is none but I shall pay:
I'll hale the Dauphin headlong from his throne:
His crown shall be the ransom of my friend;
Four of their lords I'll change for one of ours.
Farewell, my masters; to my task will I;
Bonfires in France forthwith I am to make,
To keep our great Saint George's feast withal:
Ten thousand soldiers with me I will take,
Whose bloody deeds shall make all Europe quake.

MESSENGER

So you had need; for Orleans is besieged;
The English army is grown weak and faint:
The Earl of Salisbury craveth supply,
And hardly keeps his men from mutiny,
Since they, so few, watch such a multitude.

EXETER

Remember, lords, your oaths to Henry sworn,
Either to quell the Dauphin utterly,
Or bring him in obedience to your yoke.

BEDFORD

I do remember it; and here take my leave,
To go about my preparation.

Exit

GLOUCESTER
I'll to the Tower with all the haste I can,
To view the artillery and munition;
And then I will proclaim young Henry king.

Exit

EXETER
To Eltham will I, where the young king is,
Being ordain'd his special governor,
And for his safety there I'll best devise.

Exit

BISHOP OF WINCHESTER
Each hath his place and function to attend:
I am left out; for me nothing remains.
But long I will not be Jack out of office:
The king from Eltham I intend to steal
And sit at chiefest stern of public weal.

Exeunt

SCENE II - France. Before Orleans

Sound a flourish.

Enter CHARLES, ALENCON, and REIGNIER, marching with drum and Soldiers

CHARLES
Mars his true moving, even as in the heavens
So in the earth, to this day is not known:
Late did he shine upon the English side;
Now we are victors; upon us he smiles.
What towns of any moment but we have?
At pleasure here we lie near Orleans;
Otherwhiles the famish'd English, like pale ghosts,
Faintly besiege us one hour in a month.

ALENCON
They want their porridge and their fat bull-beeves:
Either they must be dieted like mules
And have their provender tied to their mouths
Or piteous they will look, like drowned mice.

REIGNIER

Let's raise the siege: why live we idly here?
Talbot is taken, whom we wont to fear:
Remaineth none but mad-brain'd Salisbury;
And he may well in fretting spend his gall,
Nor men nor money hath he to make war.

CHARLES

Sound, sound alarum! we will rush on them.
Now for the honour of the forlorn French!
Him I forgive my death that killeth me
When he sees me go back one foot or fly.

Exeunt

Here alarum; they are beaten back by the English with great loss.

Re-enter CHARLES, ALENCON, and REIGNIER

CHARLES

Who ever saw the like? what men have I!
Dogs! cowards! dastards! I would ne'er have fled,
But that they left me 'midst my enemies.

REIGNIER

Salisbury is a desperate homicide;
He fighteth as one weary of his life.
The other lords, like lions wanting food,
Do rush upon us as their hungry prey.

ALENCON

Froissart, a countryman of ours, records,
England all Olivers and Rowlands bred,
During the time Edward the Third did reign.
More truly now may this be verified;
For none but Samsons and Goliases
It sendeth forth to skirmish. One to ten!
Lean, raw-boned rascals! who would e'er suppose
They had such courage and audacity?

CHARLES

Let's leave this town; for they are hare-brain'd slaves,
And hunger will enforce them to be more eager:
Of old I know them; rather with their teeth
The walls they'll tear down than forsake the siege.

REIGNIER

I think, by some odd gimmors or device
Their arms are set like clocks, stiff to strike on;

Else ne'er could they hold out so as they do.
By my consent, we'll even let them alone.

ALENCON
Be it so.

Enter the BASTARD OF ORLEANS

BASTARD OF ORLEANS
Where's the Prince Dauphin? I have news for him.

CHARLES
Bastard of Orleans, thrice welcome to us.

BASTARD OF ORLEANS
Methinks your looks are sad, your cheer appall'd:
Hath the late overthrow wrought this offence?
Be not dismay'd, for succor is at hand:
A holy maid hither with me I bring,
Which by a vision sent to her from heaven
Ordained is to raise this tedious siege
And drive the English forth the bounds of France.
The spirit of deep prophecy she hath,
Exceeding the nine sibyls of old Rome:
What's past and what's to come she can descry.
Speak, shall I call her in? Believe my words,
For they are certain and unfallible.

CHARLES
Go, call her in.

Exit BASTARD OF ORLEANS

But first, to try her skill,
Reignier, stand thou as Dauphin in my place:
Question her proudly; let thy looks be stern:
By this means shall we sound what skill she hath.

Re-enter the BASTARD OF ORLEANS, with JOAN LA PUCELLE

REIGNIER
Fair maid, is't thou wilt do these wondrous feats?

JOAN LA PUCELLE
Reignier, is't thou that thinkest to beguile me?
Where is the Dauphin? Come, come from behind;
I know thee well, though never seen before.
Be not amazed, there's nothing hid from me:
In private will I talk with thee apart.
Stand back, you lords, and give us leave awhile.

REIGNIER
She takes upon her bravely at first dash.

JOAN LA PUCELLE
Dauphin, I am by birth a shepherd's daughter,
My wit untrain'd in any kind of art.
Heaven and our Lady gracious hath it pleased
To shine on my contemptible estate:
Lo, whilst I waited on my tender lambs,
And to sun's parching heat display'd my cheeks,
God's mother deigned to appear to me
And in a vision full of majesty
Will'd me to leave my base vocation
And free my country from calamity:
Her aid she promised and assured success:
In complete glory she reveal'd herself;
And, whereas I was black and swart before,
With those clear rays which she infused on me
That beauty am I bless'd with which you see.
Ask me what question thou canst possible,
And I will answer unpremeditated:
My courage try by combat, if thou darest,
And thou shalt find that I exceed my sex.
Resolve on this, thou shalt be fortunate,
If thou receive me for thy warlike mate.

CHARLES
Thou hast astonish'd me with thy high terms:
Only this proof I'll of thy valour make,
In single combat thou shalt buckle with me,
And if thou vanquishest, thy words are true;
Otherwise I renounce all confidence.

JOAN LA PUCELLE
I am prepared: here is my keen-edged sword,
Deck'd with five flower-de-luces on each side;
The which at Touraine, in Saint Katharine's churchyard,
Out of a great deal of old iron I chose forth.

CHARLES
Then come, o' God's name; I fear no woman.

JOAN LA PUCELLE
And while I live, I'll ne'er fly from a man.

Here they fight, and JOAN LA PUCELLE overcomes

CHARLES
Stay, stay thy hands! thou art an Amazon
And fightest with the sword of Deborah.

JOAN LA PUCELLE
Christ's mother helps me, else I were too weak.

CHARLES
Whoe'er helps thee, 'tis thou that must help me:
Impatiently I burn with thy desire;
My heart and hands thou hast at once subdued.
Excellent Pucelle, if thy name be so,
Let me thy servant and not sovereign be:
'Tis the French Dauphin sueth to thee thus.

JOAN LA PUCELLE
I must not yield to any rites of love,
For my profession's sacred from above:
When I have chased all thy foes from hence,
Then will I think upon a recompense.

CHARLES
Meantime look gracious on thy prostrate thrall.

REIGNIER
My lord, methinks, is very long in talk.

ALENCON
Doubtless he shrives this woman to her smock;
Else ne'er could he so long protract his speech.

REIGNIER
Shall we disturb him, since he keeps no mean?

ALENCON
He may mean more than we poor men do know:
These women are shrewd tempters with their tongues.

REIGNIER
My lord, where are you? what devise you on?
Shall we give over Orleans, or no?

JOAN LA PUCELLE
Why, no, I say, distrustful recreants!
Fight till the last gasp; I will be your guard.

CHARLES
What she says I'll confirm: we'll fight it out.

JOAN LA PUCELLE
Assign'd am I to be the English scourge.
This night the siege assuredly I'll raise:
Expect Saint Martin's summer, halcyon days,
Since I have entered into these wars.
Glory is like a circle in the water,

Which never ceaseth to enlarge itself
Till by broad spreading it disperse to nought.
With Henry's death the English circle ends;
Dispersed are the glories it included.
Now am I like that proud insulting ship
Which Caesar and his fortune bare at once.

CHARLES
Was Mahomet inspired with a dove?
Thou with an eagle art inspired then.
Helen, the mother of great Constantine,
Nor yet Saint Philip's daughters, were like thee.
Bright star of Venus, fall'n down on the earth,
How may I reverently worship thee enough?

ALENCON
Leave off delays, and let us raise the siege.

REIGNIER
Woman, do what thou canst to save our honours;
Drive them from Orleans and be immortalized.

CHARLES
Presently we'll try: come, let's away about it:
No prophet will I trust, if she prove false.

Exeunt

SCENE III - London. Before the Tower

Enter GLOUCESTER, with his Serving-men in blue coats

GLOUCESTER
I am come to survey the Tower this day:
Since Henry's death, I fear, there is conveyance.
Where be these warders, that they wait not here?
Open the gates; 'tis Gloucester that calls.

FIRST WARDER
[Within] Who's there that knocks so imperiously?
First Serving-Man It is the noble Duke of Gloucester.

SECOND WARDER
[Within] Whoe'er he be, you may not be let in.
First Serving-Man Villains, answer you so the lord protector?

FIRST WARDER
[Within] The Lord protect him! so we answer him:
We do no otherwise than we are will'd.

GLOUCESTER
Who willed you? or whose will stands but mine?
There's none protector of the realm but I.
Break up the gates, I'll be your warrantize.
Shall I be flouted thus by dunghill grooms?

Gloucester's men rush at the Tower Gates, and WOODVILE the Lieutenant speaks within

WOODVILE
What noise is this? what traitors have we here?

GLOUCESTER
Lieutenant, is it you whose voice I hear?
Open the gates; here's Gloucester that would enter.

WOODVILE
Have patience, noble duke; I may not open;
The Cardinal of Winchester forbids:
From him I have express commandment
That thou nor none of thine shall be let in.

GLOUCESTER
Faint-hearted Woodvile, prizest him 'fore me?
Arrogant Winchester, that haughty prelate,
Whom Henry, our late sovereign, ne'er could brook?
Thou art no friend to God or to the king:
Open the gates, or I'll shut thee out shortly.
Serving-Men Open the gates unto the lord protector,
Or we'll burst them open, if that you come not quickly.

Enter to the Protector at the Tower Gates BISHOP OF WINCHESTER and his men in tawny coats

BISHOP OF WINCHESTER
How now, ambitious Humphry! what means this?

GLOUCESTER
Peel'd priest, dost thou command me to be shut out?

BISHOP OF WINCHESTER
I do, thou most usurping proditor,
And not protector, of the king or realm.

GLOUCESTER
Stand back, thou manifest conspirator,
Thou that contrivedst to murder our dead lord;
Thou that givest whores indulgences to sin:
I'll canvass thee in thy broad cardinal's hat,
If thou proceed in this thy insolence.

BISHOP OF WINCHESTER

Nay, stand thou back, I will not budge a foot:
This be Damascus, be thou cursed Cain,
To slay thy brother Abel, if thou wilt.

GLOUCESTER
I will not slay thee, but I'll drive thee back:
Thy scarlet robes as a child's bearing-cloth
I'll use to carry thee out of this place.

BISHOP OF WINCHESTER
Do what thou darest; I beard thee to thy face.

GLOUCESTER
What! am I dared and bearded to my face?
Draw, men, for all this privileged place;
Blue coats to tawny coats. Priest, beware your beard,
I mean to tug it and to cuff you soundly:
Under my feet I stamp thy cardinal's hat:
In spite of pope or dignities of church,
Here by the cheeks I'll drag thee up and down.

BISHOP OF WINCHESTER
Gloucester, thou wilt answer this before the pope.

GLOUCESTER
Winchester goose, I cry, a rope! a rope!
Now beat them hence; why do you let them stay?
Thee I'll chase hence, thou wolf in sheep's array.
Out, tawny coats! out, scarlet hypocrite!

Here GLOUCESTER's men beat out BISHOP OF WINCHESTER's men, and enter in the hurly-burly the MAYOR of London and his OFFICERS

MAYOR
Fie, lords! that you, being supreme magistrates,
Thus contumeliously should break the peace!

GLOUCESTER
Peace, mayor! thou know'st little of my wrongs:
Here's Beaufort, that regards nor God nor king,
Hath here distrain'd the Tower to his use.

BISHOP OF WINCHESTER
Here's Gloucester, a foe to citizens,
One that still motions war and never peace,
O'ercharging your free purses with large fines,
That seeks to overthrow religion,
Because he is protector of the realm,
And would have armour here out of the Tower,
To crown himself king and suppress the prince.

GLOUCESTER
I will not answer thee with words, but blows.

Here they skirmish again

MAYOR
Naught rests for me in this tumultuous strife
But to make open proclamation:
Come, officer; as loud as e'er thou canst,
Cry.

OFFICER
All manner of men assembled here in arms this day
against God's peace and the king's, we charge and
command you, in his highness' name, to repair to
your several dwelling-places; and not to wear,
handle, or use any sword, weapon, or dagger,
henceforward, upon pain of death.

GLOUCESTER
Cardinal, I'll be no breaker of the law:
But we shall meet, and break our minds at large.

BISHOP OF WINCHESTER
Gloucester, we will meet; to thy cost, be sure:
Thy heart-blood I will have for this day's work.

MAYOR
I'll call for clubs, if you will not away.
This cardinal's more haughty than the devil.

GLOUCESTER
Mayor, farewell: thou dost but what thou mayst.

BISHOP OF WINCHESTER
Abominable Gloucester, guard thy head;
For I intend to have it ere long.

Exeunt, severally, GLOUCESTER and BISHOP OF WINCHESTER with their Serving-men

MAYOR
See the coast clear'd, and then we will depart.
Good God, these nobles should such stomachs bear!
I myself fight not once in forty year.

Exeunt

SCENE IV. Orleans.

Enter, on the walls, a Master Gunner and his BOY

MASTER-GUNNER
Sirrah, thou know'st how Orleans is besieged,
And how the English have the suburbs won.

BOY
Father, I know; and oft have shot at them,
Howe'er unfortunate I miss'd my aim.

MASTER-GUNNER
But now thou shalt not. Be thou ruled by me:
Chief master-gunner am I of this town;
Something I must do to procure me grace.
The prince's espials have informed me
How the English, in the suburbs close intrench'd,
Wont, through a secret grate of iron bars
In yonder tower, to overpeer the city,
And thence discover how with most advantage
They may vex us with shot, or with assault.
To intercept this inconvenience,
A piece of ordnance 'gainst it I have placed;
And even these three days have I watch'd,
If I could see them.
Now do thou watch, for I can stay no longer.
If thou spy'st any, run and bring me word;
And thou shalt find me at the governor's.

Exit

BOY
Father, I warrant you; take you no care;
I'll never trouble you, if I may spy them.

Exit

Enter, on the turrets, SALISBURY and TALBOT, GLANSDALE, GARGRAVE, and others

SALISBURY
Talbot, my life, my joy, again return'd!
How wert thou handled being prisoner?
Or by what means got'st thou to be released?
Discourse, I prithee, on this turret's top.

TALBOT
The Duke of Bedford had a prisoner
Call'd the brave Lord Ponton de Santrailles;
For him was I exchanged and ransomed.
But with a baser man of arms by far
Once in contempt they would have barter'd me:
Which I, disdaining, scorn'd; and craved death,

Rather than I would be so vile esteem'd.
In fine, redeem'd I was as I desired.
But, O! the treacherous Fastolfe wounds my heart,
Whom with my bare fists I would execute,
If I now had him brought into my power.

SALISBURY
Yet tell'st thou not how thou wert entertain'd.

TALBOT
With scoffs and scorns and contumelious taunts.
In open market-place produced they me,
To be a public spectacle to all:
Here, said they, is the terror of the French,
The scarecrow that affrights our children so.
Then broke I from the officers that led me,
And with my nails digg'd stones out of the ground,
To hurl at the beholders of my shame:
My grisly countenance made others fly;
None durst come near for fear of sudden death.
In iron walls they deem'd me not secure;
So great fear of my name 'mongst them was spread,
That they supposed I could rend bars of steel,
And spurn in pieces posts of adamant:
Wherefore a guard of chosen shot I had,
That walked about me every minute-while;
And if I did but stir out of my bed,
Ready they were to shoot me to the heart.

Enter the BOY with a linstock

SALISBURY
I grieve to hear what torments you endured,
But we will be revenged sufficiently
Now it is supper-time in Orleans:
Here, through this grate, I count each one
and view the Frenchmen how they fortify:
Let us look in; the sight will much delight thee.
Sir Thomas Gargrave, and Sir William Glansdale,
Let me have your express opinions
Where is best place to make our battery next.

GARGRAVE
I think, at the north gate; for there stand lords.

GLANSDALE
And I, here, at the bulwark of the bridge.

TALBOT
For aught I see, this city must be famish'd,
Or with light skirmishes enfeebled.

Here they shoot. SALISBURY and GARGRAVE fall

SALISBURY
O Lord, have mercy on us, wretched sinners!

GARGRAVE
O Lord, have mercy on me, woful man!

TALBOT
What chance is this that suddenly hath cross'd us?
Speak, Salisbury; at least, if thou canst speak:
How farest thou, mirror of all martial men?
One of thy eyes and thy cheek's side struck off!
Accursed tower! accursed fatal hand
That hath contrived this woful tragedy!
In thirteen battles Salisbury o'ercame;
Henry the Fifth he first train'd to the wars;
Whilst any trump did sound, or drum struck up,
His sword did ne'er leave striking in the field.
Yet livest thou, Salisbury? though thy speech doth fail,
One eye thou hast, to look to heaven for grace:
The sun with one eye vieweth all the world.
Heaven, be thou gracious to none alive,
If Salisbury wants mercy at thy hands!
Bear hence his body; I will help to bury it.
Sir Thomas Gargrave, hast thou any life?
Speak unto Talbot; nay, look up to him.
Salisbury, cheer thy spirit with this comfort;
Thou shalt not die whiles--
He beckons with his hand and smiles on me.
As who should say 'When I am dead and gone,
Remember to avenge me on the French.'
Plantagenet, I will; and like thee, Nero,
Play on the lute, beholding the towns burn:
Wretched shall France be only in my name.

Here an alarum, and it thunders and lightens

What stir is this? what tumult's in the heavens?
Whence cometh this alarum and the noise?

Enter a MESSENGER

MESSENGER
My lord, my lord, the French have gathered head:
The Dauphin, with one Joan la Pucelle join'd,
A holy prophetess new risen up,
Is come with a great power to raise the siege.

Here SALISBURY lifteth himself up and groans

TALBOT
Hear, hear how dying Salisbury doth groan!
It irks his heart he cannot be revenged.
Frenchmen, I'll be a Salisbury to you:
Pucelle or puzzel, dolphin or dogfish,
Your hearts I'll stamp out with my horse's heels,
And make a quagmire of your mingled brains.
Convey me Salisbury into his tent,
And then we'll try what these dastard Frenchmen dare.

Alarum.

Exeunt

SCENE V. The Same.

Here an alarum again: and TALBOT pursueth the DAUPHIN, and driveth him: then enter JOAN LA PUCELLE, driving Englishmen before her, and exit after them then re-enter TALBOT

TALBOT
Where is my strength, my valour, and my force?
Our English troops retire, I cannot stay them:
A woman clad in armour chaseth them.

Re-enter JOAN LA PUCELLE

Here, here she comes. I'll have a bout with thee;
Devil or devil's dam, I'll conjure thee:
Blood will I draw on thee, thou art a witch,
And straightway give thy soul to him thou servest.

JOAN LA PUCELLE
Come, come, 'tis only I that must disgrace thee.

Here they fight

TALBOT
Heavens, can you suffer hell so to prevail?
My breast I'll burst with straining of my courage
And from my shoulders crack my arms asunder.
But I will chastise this high-minded strumpet.

They fight again

JOAN LA PUCELLE
Talbot, farewell; thy hour is not yet come:
I must go victual Orleans forthwith.
A short alarum; then enter the town with soldiers

O'ertake me, if thou canst; I scorn thy strength.
Go, go, cheer up thy hungry-starved men;
Help Salisbury to make his testament:
This day is ours, as many more shall be.

Exit

TALBOT
My thoughts are whirled like a potter's wheel;
I know not where I am, nor what I do;
A witch, by fear, not force, like Hannibal,
Drives back our troops and conquers as she lists:
So bees with smoke and doves with noisome stench
Are from their hives and houses driven away.
They call'd us for our fierceness English dogs;
Now, like to whelps, we crying run away.

A short alarum

Hark, countrymen! either renew the fight,
Or tear the lions out of England's coat;
Renounce your soil, give sheep in lions' stead:
Sheep run not half so treacherous from the wolf,
Or horse or oxen from the leopard,
As you fly from your oft-subdued slaves.

Alarum. Here another skirmish

It will not be: retire into your trenches:
You all consented unto Salisbury's death,
For none would strike a stroke in his revenge.
Pucelle is enter'd into Orleans,
In spite of us or aught that we could do.
O, would I were to die with Salisbury!
The shame hereof will make me hide my head.

Exit TALBOT. Alarum; retreat; flourish

SCENE VI. The same.

Enter, on the walls, JOAN LA PUCELLE, CHARLES, REIGNIER, ALENCON, and Soldiers

JOAN LA PUCELLE
Advance our waving colours on the walls;
Rescued is Orleans from the English
Thus Joan la Pucelle hath perform'd her word.

CHARLES

Divinest creature, Astraea's daughter,
How shall I honour thee for this success?
Thy promises are like Adonis' gardens
That one day bloom'd and fruitful were the next.
France, triumph in thy glorious prophetess!
Recover'd is the town of Orleans:
More blessed hap did ne'er befall our state.

REIGNIER
Why ring not out the bells aloud throughout the town?
Dauphin, command the citizens make bonfires
And feast and banquet in the open streets,
To celebrate the joy that God hath given us.

ALENCON
All France will be replete with mirth and joy,
When they shall hear how we have play'd the men.

CHARLES
'Tis Joan, not we, by whom the day is won;
For which I will divide my crown with her,
And all the priests and friars in my realm
Shall in procession sing her endless praise.
A statelier pyramis to her I'll rear
Than Rhodope's or Memphis' ever was:
In memory of her when she is dead,
Her ashes, in an urn more precious
Than the rich-jewel'd of Darius,
Transported shall be at high festivals
Before the kings and queens of France.
No longer on Saint Denis will we cry,
But Joan la Pucelle shall be France's saint.
Come in, and let us banquet royally,
After this golden day of victory.

Flourish.

Exeunt

ACT II

SCENE I. Before Orleans.

Enter a SERGEANT of a band with two SENTINELS

SERGEANT
Sirs, take your places and be vigilant:
If any noise or soldier you perceive

Near to the walls, by some apparent sign
Let us have knowledge at the court of guard.

FIRST SENTINEL
Sergeant, you shall.

Exit SERGEANT

Thus are poor servitors,
When others sleep upon their quiet beds,
Constrain'd to watch in darkness, rain and cold.

Enter TALBOT, BEDFORD, BURGUNDY, and Forces, with scaling-ladders, their drums beating a dead march

TALBOT
Lord Regent, and redoubted Burgundy,
By whose approach the regions of Artois,
Wallon and Picardy are friends to us,
This happy night the Frenchmen are secure,
Having all day caroused and banqueted:
Embrace we then this opportunity
As fitting best to quittance their deceit
Contrived by art and baleful sorcery.

BEDFORD
Coward of France! how much he wrongs his fame,
Despairing of his own arm's fortitude,
To join with witches and the help of hell!

BURGUNDY
Traitors have never other company.
But what's that Pucelle whom they term so pure?

TALBOT
A maid, they say.

BEDFORD
A maid! and be so martial!

BURGUNDY
Pray God she prove not masculine ere long,
If underneath the standard of the French
She carry armour as she hath begun.

TALBOT
Well, let them practise and converse with spirits:
God is our fortress, in whose conquering name
Let us resolve to scale their flinty bulwarks.

BEDFORD
Ascend, brave Talbot; we will follow thee.

TALBOT
Not all together: better far, I guess,
That we do make our entrance several ways;
That, if it chance the one of us do fail,
The other yet may rise against their force.

BEDFORD
Agreed: I'll to yond corner.

BURGUNDY
And I to this.

TALBOT
And here will Talbot mount, or make his grave.
Now, Salisbury, for thee, and for the right
Of English Henry, shall this night appear
How much in duty I am bound to both.

SENTINELS
Arm! arm! the enemy doth make assault!

CRY: *'St. George,' 'A Talbot.'*

The French leap over the walls in their shirts. Enter, several ways, the BASTARD OF ORLEANS, ALENCON, and REIGNIER, half ready, and half unready

ALENCON
How now, my lords! what, all unready so?

BASTARD OF ORLEANS
Unready! ay, and glad we 'scaped so well.

REIGNIER
'Twas time, I trow, to wake and leave our beds,
Hearing alarums at our chamber-doors.

ALENCON
Of all exploits since first I follow'd arms,
Ne'er heard I of a warlike enterprise
More venturous or desperate than this.

BASTARD OF ORLEANS
I think this Talbot be a fiend of hell.

REIGNIER
If not of hell, the heavens, sure, favour him.

ALENCON

Here cometh Charles: I marvel how he sped.

BASTARD OF ORLEANS
Tut, holy Joan was his defensive guard.

Enter CHARLES and JOAN LA PUCELLE

CHARLES
Is this thy cunning, thou deceitful dame?
Didst thou at first, to flatter us withal,
Make us partakers of a little gain,
That now our loss might be ten times so much?

JOAN LA PUCELLE
Wherefore is Charles impatient with his friend!
At all times will you have my power alike?
Sleeping or waking must I still prevail,
Or will you blame and lay the fault on me?
Improvident soldiers! had your watch been good,
This sudden mischief never could have fall'n.

CHARLES
Duke of Alencon, this was your default,
That, being captain of the watch to-night,
Did look no better to that weighty charge.

ALENCON
Had all your quarters been as safely kept
As that whereof I had the government,
We had not been thus shamefully surprised.

BASTARD OF ORLEANS
Mine was secure.

REIGNIER
And so was mine, my lord.

CHARLES
And, for myself, most part of all this night,
Within her quarter and mine own precinct
I was employ'd in passing to and fro,
About relieving of the sentinels:
Then how or which way should they first break in?

JOAN LA PUCELLE
Question, my lords, no further of the case,
How or which way: 'tis sure they found some place
But weakly guarded, where the breach was made.
And now there rests no other shift but this;
To gather our soldiers, scatter'd and dispersed,
And lay new platforms to endamage them.

Alarum.

Enter an English SOLDIER, crying 'A Talbot! a Talbot!'

They fly, leaving their clothes behind

SOLDIER
I'll be so bold to take what they have left.
The cry of Talbot serves me for a sword;
For I have loaden me with many spoils,
Using no other weapon but his name.

Exit

SCENE II. Orleans. Within the town.

Enter TALBOT, BEDFORD, BURGUNDY, a Captain, and others

BEDFORD
The day begins to break, and night is fled,
Whose pitchy mantle over-veil'd the earth.
Here sound retreat, and cease our hot pursuit.

Retreat sounded

TALBOT
Bring forth the body of old Salisbury,
And here advance it in the market-place,
The middle centre of this cursed town.
Now have I paid my vow unto his soul;
For every drop of blood was drawn from him,
There hath at least five Frenchmen died tonight.
And that hereafter ages may behold
What ruin happen'd in revenge of him,
Within their chiefest temple I'll erect
A tomb, wherein his corpse shall be interr'd:
Upon the which, that every one may read,
Shall be engraved the sack of Orleans,
The treacherous manner of his mournful death
And what a terror he had been to France.
But, lords, in all our bloody massacre,
I muse we met not with the Dauphin's grace,
His new-come champion, virtuous Joan of Arc,
Nor any of his false confederates.

BEDFORD

'Tis thought, Lord Talbot, when the fight began,
Roused on the sudden from their drowsy beds,
They did amongst the troops of armed men
Leap o'er the walls for refuge in the field.

BURGUNDY
Myself, as far as I could well discern
For smoke and dusky vapours of the night,
Am sure I scared the Dauphin and his trull,
When arm in arm they both came swiftly running,
Like to a pair of loving turtle-doves
That could not live asunder day or night.
After that things are set in order here,
We'll follow them with all the power we have.

Enter a MESSENGER

MESSENGER
All hail, my lords! which of this princely train
Call ye the warlike Talbot, for his acts
So much applauded through the realm of France?

TALBOT
Here is the Talbot: who would speak with him?

MESSENGER
The virtuous lady, Countess of Auvergne,
With modesty admiring thy renown,
By me entreats, great lord, thou wouldst vouchsafe
To visit her poor castle where she lies,
That she may boast she hath beheld the man
Whose glory fills the world with loud report.

BURGUNDY
Is it even so? Nay, then, I see our wars
Will turn unto a peaceful comic sport,
When ladies crave to be encounter'd with.
You may not, my lord, despise her gentle suit.

TALBOT
Ne'er trust me then; for when a world of men
Could not prevail with all their oratory,
Yet hath a woman's kindness over-ruled:
And therefore tell her I return great thanks,
And in submission will attend on her.
Will not your honours bear me company?

BEDFORD
No, truly; it is more than manners will:
And I have heard it said, unbidden guests
Are often welcomest when they are gone.

TALBOT
Well then, alone, since there's no remedy,
I mean to prove this lady's courtesy.
Come hither, captain.

Whispers

You perceive my mind?

CAPTAIN
I do, my lord, and mean accordingly.

Exeunt

SCENE III. Auvergne. The Countess's Castle.

Enter the COUNTESS and her PORTER

COUNTESS OF AUVERGNE
Porter, remember what I gave in charge;
And when you have done so, bring the keys to me.

PORTER
Madam, I will.

Exit

COUNTESS OF AUVERGNE
The plot is laid: if all things fall out right,
I shall as famous be by this exploit
As Scythian Tomyris by Cyrus' death.
Great is the rumor of this dreadful knight,
And his achievements of no less account:
Fain would mine eyes be witness with mine ears,
To give their censure of these rare reports.

Enter MESSENGER and TALBOT

MESSENGER
Madam,
According as your ladyship desired,
By message craved, so is Lord Talbot come.

COUNTESS OF AUVERGNE
And he is welcome. What! is this the man?

MESSENGER
Madam, it is.

COUNTESS OF AUVERGNE
Is this the scourge of France?
Is this the Talbot, so much fear'd abroad
That with his name the mothers still their babes?
I see report is fabulous and false:
I thought I should have seen some Hercules,
A second Hector, for his grim aspect,
And large proportion of his strong-knit limbs.
Alas, this is a child, a silly dwarf!
It cannot be this weak and writhled shrimp
Should strike such terror to his enemies.

TALBOT
Madam, I have been bold to trouble you;
But since your ladyship is not at leisure,
I'll sort some other time to visit you.

COUNTESS OF AUVERGNE
What means he now? Go ask him whither he goes.

MESSENGER
Stay, my Lord Talbot; for my lady craves
To know the cause of your abrupt departure.

TALBOT
Marry, for that she's in a wrong belief,
I go to certify her Talbot's here.

Re-enter PORTER with keys

COUNTESS OF AUVERGNE
If thou be he, then art thou prisoner.

TALBOT
Prisoner! to whom?

COUNTESS OF AUVERGNE
To me, blood-thirsty lord;
And for that cause I trained thee to my house.
Long time thy shadow hath been thrall to me,
For in my gallery thy picture hangs:
But now the substance shall endure the like,
And I will chain these legs and arms of thine,
That hast by tyranny these many years
Wasted our country, slain our citizens
And sent our sons and husbands captivate.

TALBOT
Ha, ha, ha!

COUNTESS OF AUVERGNE
Laughest thou, wretch? thy mirth shall turn to moan.

TALBOT
I laugh to see your ladyship so fond
To think that you have aught but Talbot's shadow
Whereon to practise your severity.

COUNTESS OF AUVERGNE
Why, art not thou the man?

TALBOT
I am indeed.

COUNTESS OF AUVERGNE
Then have I substance too.

TALBOT
No, no, I am but shadow of myself:
You are deceived, my substance is not here;
For what you see is but the smallest part
And least proportion of humanity:
I tell you, madam, were the whole frame here,
It is of such a spacious lofty pitch,
Your roof were not sufficient to contain't.

COUNTESS OF AUVERGNE
This is a riddling merchant for the nonce;
He will be here, and yet he is not here:
How can these contrarieties agree?

TALBOT
That will I show you presently.

Winds his horn. Drums strike up: a peal of ordnance.

Enter SOLDIERS

How say you, madam? are you now persuaded
That Talbot is but shadow of himself?
These are his substance, sinews, arms and strength,
With which he yoketh your rebellious necks,
Razeth your cities and subverts your towns
And in a moment makes them desolate.

COUNTESS OF AUVERGNE
Victorious Talbot! pardon my abuse:
I find thou art no less than fame hath bruited
And more than may be gather'd by thy shape.
Let my presumption not provoke thy wrath;

For I am sorry that with reverence
I did not entertain thee as thou art.

TALBOT
Be not dismay'd, fair lady; nor misconstrue
The mind of Talbot, as you did mistake
The outward composition of his body.
What you have done hath not offended me;
Nor other satisfaction do I crave,
But only, with your patience, that we may
Taste of your wine and see what cates you have;
For soldiers' stomachs always serve them well.

COUNTESS OF AUVERGNE
With all my heart, and think me honoured
To feast so great a warrior in my house.

Exeunt

SCENE IV. London. The Temple-garden.

Enter the Earls of SOMERSET, SUFFOLK, and WARWICK; RICHARD PLANTAGENET, VERNON, and another LAWYER

RICHARD PLANTAGENET
Great lords and gentlemen, what means this silence?
Dare no man answer in a case of truth?

SUFFOLK
Within the Temple-hall we were too loud;
The garden here is more convenient.

RICHARD PLANTAGENET
Then say at once if I maintain'd the truth;
Or else was wrangling Somerset in the error?

SUFFOLK
Faith, I have been a truant in the law,
And never yet could frame my will to it;
And therefore frame the law unto my will.

SOMERSET
Judge you, my Lord of Warwick, then, between us.

WARWICK
Between two hawks, which flies the higher pitch;
Between two dogs, which hath the deeper mouth;
Between two blades, which bears the better temper:
Between two horses, which doth bear him best;

Between two girls, which hath the merriest eye;
I have perhaps some shallow spirit of judgement;
But in these nice sharp quillets of the law,
Good faith, I am no wiser than a daw.

RICHARD PLANTAGENET
Tut, tut, here is a mannerly forbearance:
The truth appears so naked on my side
That any purblind eye may find it out.

SOMERSET
And on my side it is so well apparell'd,
So clear, so shining and so evident
That it will glimmer through a blind man's eye.

RICHARD PLANTAGENET
Since you are tongue-tied and so loath to speak,
In dumb significants proclaim your thoughts:
Let him that is a true-born gentleman
And stands upon the honour of his birth,
If he suppose that I have pleaded truth,
From off this brier pluck a white rose with me.

SOMERSET
Let him that is no coward nor no flatterer,
But dare maintain the party of the truth,
Pluck a red rose from off this thorn with me.

WARWICK
I love no colours, and without all colour
Of base insinuating flattery
I pluck this white rose with Plantagenet.

SUFFOLK
I pluck this red rose with young Somerset
And say withal I think he held the right.

VERNON
Stay, lords and gentlemen, and pluck no more,
Till you conclude that he upon whose side
The fewest roses are cropp'd from the tree
Shall yield the other in the right opinion.

SOMERSET
Good Master Vernon, it is well objected:
If I have fewest, I subscribe in silence.

RICHARD PLANTAGENET
And I.

VERNON

Then for the truth and plainness of the case.
I pluck this pale and maiden blossom here,
Giving my verdict on the white rose side.

SOMERSET
Prick not your finger as you pluck it off,
Lest bleeding you do paint the white rose red
And fall on my side so, against your will.

VERNON
If I my lord, for my opinion bleed,
Opinion shall be surgeon to my hurt
And keep me on the side where still I am.

SOMERSET
Well, well, come on: who else?

LAWYER
Unless my study and my books be false,
The argument you held was wrong in you:

To SOMERSET

In sign whereof I pluck a white rose too.

RICHARD PLANTAGENET
Now, Somerset, where is your argument?

SOMERSET
Here in my scabbard, meditating that
Shall dye your white rose in a bloody red.

RICHARD PLANTAGENET
Meantime your cheeks do counterfeit our roses;
For pale they look with fear, as witnessing
The truth on our side.

SOMERSET
No, Plantagenet,
'Tis not for fear but anger that thy cheeks
Blush for pure shame to counterfeit our roses,
And yet thy tongue will not confess thy error.

RICHARD PLANTAGENET
Hath not thy rose a canker, Somerset?

SOMERSET
Hath not thy rose a thorn, Plantagenet?

RICHARD PLANTAGENET

Ay, sharp and piercing, to maintain his truth;
Whiles thy consuming canker eats his falsehood.

SOMERSET
Well, I'll find friends to wear my bleeding roses,
That shall maintain what I have said is true,
Where false Plantagenet dare not be seen.

RICHARD PLANTAGENET
Now, by this maiden blossom in my hand,
I scorn thee and thy fashion, peevish boy.

SUFFOLK
Turn not thy scorns this way, Plantagenet.

RICHARD PLANTAGENET
Proud Pole, I will, and scorn both him and thee.

SUFFOLK
I'll turn my part thereof into thy throat.

SOMERSET
Away, away, good William de la Pole!
We grace the yeoman by conversing with him.

WARWICK
Now, by God's will, thou wrong'st him, Somerset;
His grandfather was Lionel Duke of Clarence,
Third son to the third Edward King of England:
Spring crestless yeomen from so deep a root?

RICHARD PLANTAGENET
He bears him on the place's privilege,
Or durst not, for his craven heart, say thus.

SOMERSET
By him that made me, I'll maintain my words
On any plot of ground in Christendom.
Was not thy father, Richard Earl of Cambridge,
For treason executed in our late king's days?
And, by his treason, stand'st not thou attainted,
Corrupted, and exempt from ancient gentry?
His trespass yet lives guilty in thy blood;
And, till thou be restored, thou art a yeoman.

RICHARD PLANTAGENET
My father was attached, not attainted,
Condemn'd to die for treason, but no traitor;
And that I'll prove on better men than Somerset,
Were growing time once ripen'd to my will.
For your partaker Pole and you yourself,

I'll note you in my book of memory,
To scourge you for this apprehension:
Look to it well and say you are well warn'd.

SOMERSET
Ah, thou shalt find us ready for thee still;
And know us by these colours for thy foes,
For these my friends in spite of thee shall wear.

RICHARD PLANTAGENET
And, by my soul, this pale and angry rose,
As cognizance of my blood-drinking hate,
Will I for ever and my faction wear,
Until it wither with me to my grave
Or flourish to the height of my degree.

SUFFOLK
Go forward and be choked with thy ambition!
And so farewell until I meet thee next.

Exit

SOMERSET
Have with thee, Pole. Farewell, ambitious Richard.

Exit

RICHARD PLANTAGENET
How I am braved and must perforce endure it!

WARWICK
This blot that they object against your house
Shall be wiped out in the next parliament
Call'd for the truce of Winchester and Gloucester;
And if thou be not then created York,
I will not live to be accounted Warwick.
Meantime, in signal of my love to thee,
Against proud Somerset and William Pole,
Will I upon thy party wear this rose:
And here I prophesy: this brawl to-day,
Grown to this faction in the Temple-garden,
Shall send between the red rose and the white
A thousand souls to death and deadly night.

RICHARD PLANTAGENET
Good Master Vernon, I am bound to you,
That you on my behalf would pluck a flower.

VERNON
In your behalf still will I wear the same.

LAWYER
And so will I.

RICHARD PLANTAGENET
Thanks, gentle sir.
Come, let us four to dinner: I dare say
This quarrel will drink blood another day.

Exeunt

SCENE V. The Tower of London.

Enter MORTIMER, brought in a chair, and GAOLERS

MORTIMER
Kind keepers of my weak decaying age,
Let dying Mortimer here rest himself.
Even like a man new haled from the rack,
So fare my limbs with long imprisonment.
And these grey locks, the pursuivants of death,
Nestor-like aged in an age of care,
Argue the end of Edmund Mortimer.
These eyes, like lamps whose wasting oil is spent,
Wax dim, as drawing to their exigent;
Weak shoulders, overborne with burthening grief,
And pithless arms, like to a wither'd vine
That droops his sapless branches to the ground;
Yet are these feet, whose strengthless stay is numb,
Unable to support this lump of clay,
Swift-winged with desire to get a grave,
As witting I no other comfort have.
But tell me, keeper, will my nephew come?

FIRST GAOLER
Richard Plantagenet, my lord, will come:
We sent unto the Temple, unto his chamber;
And answer was return'd that he will come.
MORTIMER
Enough: my soul shall then be satisfied.
Poor gentleman! his wrong doth equal mine.
Since Henry Monmouth first began to reign,
Before whose glory I was great in arms,
This loathsome sequestration have I had:
And even since then hath Richard been obscured,
Deprived of honour and inheritance.
But now the arbitrator of despairs,
Just death, kind umpire of men's miseries,
With sweet enlargement doth dismiss me hence:

I would his troubles likewise were expired,
That so he might recover what was lost.

Enter RICHARD PLANTAGENET

FIRST GAOLER
My lord, your loving nephew now is come.

MORTIMER
Richard Plantagenet, my friend, is he come?

RICHARD PLANTAGENET
Ay, noble uncle, thus ignobly used,
Your nephew, late despised Richard, comes.

MORTIMER
Direct mine arms I may embrace his neck,
And in his bosom spend my latter gasp:
O, tell me when my lips do touch his cheeks,
That I may kindly give one fainting kiss.
And now declare, sweet stem from York's great stock,
Why didst thou say, of late thou wert despised?

RICHARD PLANTAGENET
First, lean thine aged back against mine arm;
And, in that ease, I'll tell thee my disease.
This day, in argument upon a case,
Some words there grew 'twixt Somerset and me;
Among which terms he used his lavish tongue
And did upbraid me with my father's death:
Which obloquy set bars before my tongue,
Else with the like I had requited him.
Therefore, good uncle, for my father's sake,
In honour of a true Plantagenet
And for alliance sake, declare the cause
My father, Earl of Cambridge, lost his head.

MORTIMER
That cause, fair nephew, that imprison'd me
And hath detain'd me all my flowering youth
Within a loathsome dungeon, there to pine,
Was cursed instrument of his decease.

RICHARD PLANTAGENET
Discover more at large what cause that was,
For I am ignorant and cannot guess.

MORTIMER
I will, if that my fading breath permit
And death approach not ere my tale be done.
Henry the Fourth, grandfather to this king,

Deposed his nephew Richard, Edward's son,
The first-begotten and the lawful heir,
Of Edward king, the third of that descent:
During whose reign the Percies of the north,
Finding his usurpation most unjust,
Endeavor'd my advancement to the throne:
The reason moved these warlike lords to this
Was, for that--young King Richard thus removed,
Leaving no heir begotten of his body--
I was the next by birth and parentage;
For by my mother I derived am
From Lionel Duke of Clarence, the third son
To King Edward the Third; whereas he
From John of Gaunt doth bring his pedigree,
Being but fourth of that heroic line.
But mark: as in this haughty attempt
They laboured to plant the rightful heir,
I lost my liberty and they their lives.
Long after this, when Henry the Fifth,
Succeeding his father Bolingbroke, did reign,
Thy father, Earl of Cambridge, then derived
From famous Edmund Langley, Duke of York,
Marrying my sister that thy mother was,
Again in pity of my hard distress
Levied an army, weening to redeem
And have install'd me in the diadem:
But, as the rest, so fell that noble earl
And was beheaded. Thus the Mortimers,
In whom the tide rested, were suppress'd.

RICHARD PLANTAGENET
Of which, my lord, your honour is the last.

MORTIMER
True; and thou seest that I no issue have
And that my fainting words do warrant death;
Thou art my heir; the rest I wish thee gather:
But yet be wary in thy studious care.

RICHARD PLANTAGENET
Thy grave admonishments prevail with me:
But yet, methinks, my father's execution
Was nothing less than bloody tyranny.

MORTIMER
With silence, nephew, be thou politic:
Strong-fixed is the house of Lancaster,
And like a mountain, not to be removed.
But now thy uncle is removing hence:

As princes do their courts, when they are cloy'd
With long continuance in a settled place.

RICHARD PLANTAGENET
O, uncle, would some part of my young years
Might but redeem the passage of your age!

MORTIMER
Thou dost then wrong me, as that slaughterer doth
Which giveth many wounds when one will kill.
Mourn not, except thou sorrow for my good;
Only give order for my funeral:
And so farewell, and fair be all thy hopes
And prosperous be thy life in peace and war!

Dies

RICHARD PLANTAGENET
And peace, no war, befall thy parting soul!
In prison hast thou spent a pilgrimage
And like a hermit overpass'd thy days.
Well, I will lock his counsel in my breast;
And what I do imagine let that rest.
Keepers, convey him hence, and I myself
Will see his burial better than his life.

Exeunt GAOLERS, bearing out the body of MORTIMER

Here dies the dusky torch of Mortimer,
Choked with ambition of the meaner sort:
And for those wrongs, those bitter injuries,
Which Somerset hath offer'd to my house:
I doubt not but with honour to redress;
And therefore haste I to the parliament,
Either to be restored to my blood,
Or make my ill the advantage of my good.

Exit

ACT III

SCENE I. London. The Parliament-house.

Flourish.

Enter KING HENRY VI, EXETER, GLOUCESTER, WARWICK, SOMERSET, and SUFFOLK; the BISHOP OF WINCHESTER, RICHARD PLANTAGENET, and others. GLOUCESTER offers to put up a bill; BISHOP OF WINCHESTER snatches it, and tears it

BISHOP OF WINCHESTER
Comest thou with deep premeditated lines,
With written pamphlets studiously devised,
Humphrey of Gloucester? If thou canst accuse,
Or aught intend'st to lay unto my charge,
Do it without invention, suddenly;
As I with sudden and extemporal speech
Purpose to answer what thou canst object.

GLOUCESTER
Presumptuous priest! this place commands my patience,
Or thou shouldst find thou hast dishonour'd me.
Think not, although in writing I preferr'd
The manner of thy vile outrageous crimes,
That therefore I have forged, or am not able
Verbatim to rehearse the method of my pen:
No, prelate; such is thy audacious wickedness,
Thy lewd, pestiferous and dissentious pranks,
As very infants prattle of thy pride.
Thou art a most pernicious usurer,
Forward by nature, enemy to peace;
Lascivious, wanton, more than well beseems
A man of thy profession and degree;
And for thy treachery, what's more manifest?
In that thou laid'st a trap to take my life,
As well at London bridge as at the Tower.
Beside, I fear me, if thy thoughts were sifted,
The king, thy sovereign, is not quite exempt
From envious malice of thy swelling heart.

BISHOP OF WINCHESTER
Gloucester, I do defy thee. Lords, vouchsafe
To give me hearing what I shall reply.
If I were covetous, ambitious or perverse,
As he will have me, how am I so poor?
Or how haps it I seek not to advance
Or raise myself, but keep my wonted calling?
And for dissension, who preferreth peace
More than I do?--except I be provoked.
No, my good lords, it is not that offends;
It is not that that hath incensed the duke:
It is, because no one should sway but he;
No one but he should be about the king;
And that engenders thunder in his breast
And makes him roar these accusations forth.
But he shall know I am as good—

GLOUCESTER
As good!
Thou bastard of my grandfather!

BISHOP OF WINCHESTER
Ay, lordly sir; for what are you, I pray,
But one imperious in another's throne?

GLOUCESTER
Am I not protector, saucy priest?

BISHOP OF WINCHESTER
And am not I a prelate of the church?

GLOUCESTER
Yes, as an outlaw in a castle keeps
And useth it to patronage his theft.

BISHOP OF WINCHESTER
Unreverent Gloster!
GLOUCESTER
Thou art reverent
Touching thy spiritual function, not thy life.

BISHOP OF WINCHESTER
Rome shall remedy this.

WARWICK
Roam thither, then.

SOMERSET
My lord, it were your duty to forbear.

WARWICK
Ay, see the bishop be not overborne.

SOMERSET
Methinks my lord should be religious
And know the office that belongs to such.

WARWICK
Methinks his lordship should be humbler;
it fitteth not a prelate so to plead.

SOMERSET
Yes, when his holy state is touch'd so near.

WARWICK
State holy or unhallow'd, what of that?
Is not his grace protector to the king?

RICHARD PLANTAGENET
[Aside] Plantagenet, I see, must hold his tongue,
Lest it be said 'Speak, sirrah, when you should;

Must your bold verdict enter talk with lords?'
Else would I have a fling at Winchester.

KING HENRY VI
Uncles of Gloucester and of Winchester,
The special watchmen of our English weal,
I would prevail, if prayers might prevail,
To join your hearts in love and amity.
O, what a scandal is it to our crown,
That two such noble peers as ye should jar!
Believe me, lords, my tender years can tell
Civil dissension is a viperous worm
That gnaws the bowels of the commonwealth.

A noise within, 'Down with the tawny-coats!'

What tumult's this?

WARWICK
An uproar, I dare warrant,
Begun through malice of the bishop's men.

A noise again, 'Stones! stones!' Enter MAYOR

MAYOR
O, my good lords, and virtuous Henry,
Pity the city of London, pity us!
The bishop and the Duke of Gloucester's men,
Forbidden late to carry any weapon,
Have fill'd their pockets full of pebble stones
And banding themselves in contrary parts
Do pelt so fast at one another's pate
That many have their giddy brains knock'd out:
Our windows are broke down in every street
And we for fear compell'd to shut our shops.

Enter Serving-men, in skirmish, with bloody pates

KING HENRY VI
We charge you, on allegiance to ourself,
To hold your slaughtering hands and keep the peace.
Pray, uncle Gloucester, mitigate this strife.
First Serving-man Nay, if we be forbidden stones,
We'll fall to it with our teeth.
Second Serving-man Do what ye dare, we are as resolute.

Skirmish again

GLOUCESTER
You of my household, leave this peevish broil
And set this unaccustom'd fight aside.

Third Serving-man My lord, we know your grace to be a man
Just and upright; and, for your royal birth,
Inferior to none but to his majesty:
And ere that we will suffer such a prince,
So kind a father of the commonweal,
To be disgraced by an inkhorn mate,
We and our wives and children all will fight
And have our bodies slaughtered by thy foes.
First Serving-man Ay, and the very parings of our nails
Shall pitch a field when we are dead.

Begin again

GLOUCESTER
Stay, stay, I say!
And if you love me, as you say you do,
Let me persuade you to forbear awhile.

KING HENRY VI
O, how this discord doth afflict my soul!
Can you, my Lord of Winchester, behold
My sighs and tears and will not once relent?
Who should be pitiful, if you be not?
Or who should study to prefer a peace.
If holy churchmen take delight in broils?

WARWICK
Yield, my lord protector; yield, Winchester;
Except you mean with obstinate repulse
To slay your sovereign and destroy the realm.
You see what mischief and what murder too
Hath been enacted through your enmity;
Then be at peace except ye thirst for blood.

BISHOP OF WINCHESTER
He shall submit, or I will never yield.

GLOUCESTER
Compassion on the king commands me stoop;
Or I would see his heart out, ere the priest
Should ever get that privilege of me.

WARWICK
Behold, my Lord of Winchester, the duke
Hath banish'd moody discontented fury,
As by his smoothed brows it doth appear:
Why look you still so stern and tragical?

GLOUCESTER
Here, Winchester, I offer thee my hand.

KING HENRY VI

Fie, uncle Beaufort! I have heard you preach
That malice was a great and grievous sin;
And will not you maintain the thing you teach,
But prove a chief offender in the same?

WARWICK

Sweet king! the bishop hath a kindly gird.
For shame, my lord of Winchester, relent!
What, shall a child instruct you what to do?

BISHOP OF WINCHESTER

Well, Duke of Gloucester, I will yield to thee;
Love for thy love and hand for hand I give.

GLOUCESTER

[Aside] Ay, but, I fear me, with a hollow heart.--
See here, my friends and loving countrymen,
This token serveth for a flag of truce
Betwixt ourselves and all our followers:
So help me God, as I dissemble not!

BISHOP OF WINCHESTER

[Aside] So help me God, as I intend it not!

KING HENRY VI

O, loving uncle, kind Duke of Gloucester,
How joyful am I made by this contract!
Away, my masters! trouble us no more;
But join in friendship, as your lords have done.
First Serving-man Content: I'll to the surgeon's.
Second Serving-man And so will I.
Third Serving-man And I will see what physic the tavern affords.

Exeunt Serving-men, MAYOR, & c

WARWICK

Accept this scroll, most gracious sovereign,
Which in the right of Richard Plantagenet
We do exhibit to your majesty.

GLOUCESTER

Well urged, my Lord of Warwick: or sweet prince,
And if your grace mark every circumstance,
You have great reason to do Richard right;
Especially for those occasions
At Eltham Place I told your majesty.

KING HENRY VI

And those occasions, uncle, were of force:
Therefore, my loving lords, our pleasure is
That Richard be restored to his blood.

WARWICK
Let Richard be restored to his blood;
So shall his father's wrongs be recompensed.

BISHOP OF WINCHESTER
As will the rest, so willeth Winchester.

KING HENRY VI
If Richard will be true, not that alone
But all the whole inheritance I give
That doth belong unto the house of York,
From whence you spring by lineal descent.

RICHARD PLANTAGENET
Thy humble servant vows obedience
And humble service till the point of death.

KING HENRY VI
Stoop then and set your knee against my foot;
And, in reguerdon of that duty done,
I gird thee with the valiant sword of York:
Rise Richard, like a true Plantagenet,
And rise created princely Duke of York.

RICHARD PLANTAGENET
And so thrive Richard as thy foes may fall!
And as my duty springs, so perish they
That grudge one thought against your majesty!

ALL
Welcome, high prince, the mighty Duke of York!

SOMERSET
[Aside] Perish, base prince, ignoble Duke of York!

GLOUCESTER
Now will it best avail your majesty
To cross the seas and to be crown'd in France:
The presence of a king engenders love
Amongst his subjects and his loyal friends,
As it disanimates his enemies.

KING HENRY VI
When Gloucester says the word, King Henry goes;
For friendly counsel cuts off many foes.

GLOUCESTER

Your ships already are in readiness.

Sennet.

Flourish.

Exeunt all but EXETER

EXETER
Ay, we may march in England or in France,
Not seeing what is likely to ensue.
This late dissension grown betwixt the peers
Burns under feigned ashes of forged love
And will at last break out into a flame:
As fester'd members rot but by degree,
Till bones and flesh and sinews fall away,
So will this base and envious discord breed.
And now I fear that fatal prophecy
Which in the time of Henry named the Fifth
Was in the mouth of every sucking babe;
That Henry born at Monmouth should win all
And Henry born at Windsor lose all:
Which is so plain that Exeter doth wish
His days may finish ere that hapless time.

Exit

SCENE II. France. Before Rouen.

Enter JOAN LA PUCELLE disguised, with four SOLDIERS with sacks upon their backs

JOAN LA PUCELLE
These are the city gates, the gates of Rouen,
Through which our policy must make a breach:
Take heed, be wary how you place your words;
Talk like the vulgar sort of market men
That come to gather money for their corn.
If we have entrance, as I hope we shall,
And that we find the slothful watch but weak,
I'll by a sign give notice to our friends,
That Charles the Dauphin may encounter them.

FIRST SOLDIER
Our sacks shall be a mean to sack the city,
And we be lords and rulers over Rouen;
Therefore we'll knock.

Knocks

WATCH
[Within] Qui est la?

JOAN LA PUCELLE
Paysans, pauvres gens de France;
Poor market folks that come to sell their corn.

WATCH
Enter, go in; the market bell is rung.

JOAN LA PUCELLE
Now, Rouen, I'll shake thy bulwarks to the ground.

Exeunt

Enter CHARLES, the BASTARD OF ORLEANS, ALENCON, REIGNIER, and forces

CHARLES
Saint Denis bless this happy stratagem!
And once again we'll sleep secure in Rouen.

BASTARD OF ORLEANS
Here enter'd Pucelle and her practisants;
Now she is there, how will she specify
Where is the best and safest passage in?

REIGNIER
By thrusting out a torch from yonder tower;
Which, once discern'd, shows that her meaning is,
No way to that, for weakness, which she enter'd.

Enter JOAN LA PUCELLE on the top, thrusting out a torch burning

JOAN LA PUCELLE
Behold, this is the happy wedding torch
That joineth Rouen unto her countrymen,
But burning fatal to the Talbotites!

Exit

BASTARD OF ORLEANS
See, noble Charles, the beacon of our friend;
The burning torch in yonder turret stands.

CHARLES
Now shine it like a comet of revenge,
A prophet to the fall of all our foes!

REIGNIER

Defer no time, delays have dangerous ends;
Enter, and cry 'The Dauphin!' presently,
And then do execution on the watch.

Alarum.

Exeunt

An alarum.

Enter TALBOT in an excursion

TALBOT
France, thou shalt rue this treason with thy tears,
If Talbot but survive thy treachery.
Pucelle, that witch, that damned sorceress,
Hath wrought this hellish mischief unawares,
That hardly we escaped the pride of France.

Exit

An alarum: excursions. BEDFORD, brought in sick in a chair.

Enter TALBOT and BURGUNDY without: within JOAN LA PUCELLE, CHARLES, BASTARD OF ORLEANS, ALENCON, and REIGNIER, on the walls

JOAN LA PUCELLE
Good morrow, gallants! want ye corn for bread?
I think the Duke of Burgundy will fast
Before he'll buy again at such a rate:
'Twas full of darnel; do you like the taste?

BURGUNDY
Scoff on, vile fiend and shameless courtezan!
I trust ere long to choke thee with thine own
And make thee curse the harvest of that corn.

CHARLES
Your grace may starve perhaps before that time.

BEDFORD
O, let no words, but deeds, revenge this treason!

JOAN LA PUCELLE
What will you do, good grey-beard? break a lance,
And run a tilt at death within a chair?

TALBOT
Foul fiend of France, and hag of all despite,
Encompass'd with thy lustful paramours!
Becomes it thee to taunt his valiant age

And twit with cowardice a man half dead?
Damsel, I'll have a bout with you again,
Or else let Talbot perish with this shame.

JOAN LA PUCELLE
Are ye so hot, sir? yet, Pucelle, hold thy peace;
If Talbot do but thunder, rain will follow.

The English whisper together in council

God speed the parliament! who shall be the speaker?

TALBOT
Dare ye come forth and meet us in the field?

JOAN LA PUCELLE
Belike your lordship takes us then for fools,
To try if that our own be ours or no.

TALBOT
I speak not to that railing Hecate,
But unto thee, Alencon, and the rest;
Will ye, like soldiers, come and fight it out?

ALENCON
Signior, no.

TALBOT
Signior, hang! base muleters of France!
Like peasant foot-boys do they keep the walls
And dare not take up arms like gentlemen.

JOAN LA PUCELLE
Away, captains! let's get us from the walls;
For Talbot means no goodness by his looks.
God be wi' you, my lord! we came but to tell you
That we are here.

Exeunt from the walls

TALBOT
And there will we be too, ere it be long,
Or else reproach be Talbot's greatest fame!
Vow, Burgundy, by honour of thy house,
Prick'd on by public wrongs sustain'd in France,
Either to get the town again or die:
And I, as sure as English Henry lives
And as his father here was conqueror,
As sure as in this late-betrayed town
Great Coeur-de-lion's heart was buried,
So sure I swear to get the town or die.

BURGUNDY
My vows are equal partners with thy vows.

TALBOT
But, ere we go, regard this dying prince,
The valiant Duke of Bedford. Come, my lord,
We will bestow you in some better place,
Fitter for sickness and for crazy age.

BEDFORD
Lord Talbot, do not so dishonour me:
Here will I sit before the walls of Rouen
And will be partner of your weal or woe.

BURGUNDY
Courageous Bedford, let us now persuade you.

BEDFORD
Not to be gone from hence; for once I read
That stout Pendragon in his litter sick
Came to the field and vanquished his foes:
Methinks I should revive the soldiers' hearts,
Because I ever found them as myself.

TALBOT
Undaunted spirit in a dying breast!
Then be it so: heavens keep old Bedford safe!
And now no more ado, brave Burgundy,
But gather we our forces out of hand
And set upon our boasting enemy.

Exeunt all but BEDFORD and Attendants

An alarum: excursions. Enter FASTOLFE and a Captain

CAPTAIN
Whither away, Sir John Fastolfe, in such haste?

FASTOLFE
Whither away! to save myself by flight:
We are like to have the overthrow again.

CAPTAIN
What! will you fly, and leave Lord Talbot?

FASTOLFE
Ay,
All the Talbots in the world, to save my life!

Exit

CAPTAIN
Cowardly knight! ill fortune follow thee!

Exit

Retreat: excursions. JOAN LA PUCELLE, ALENCON, and CHARLES fly

BEDFORD
Now, quiet soul, depart when heaven please,
For I have seen our enemies' overthrow.
What is the trust or strength of foolish man?
They that of late were daring with their scoffs
Are glad and fain by flight to save themselves.

BEDFORD dies, and is carried in by two in his chair

An alarum.

Re-enter TALBOT, BURGUNDY, and the rest

TALBOT
Lost, and recover'd in a day again!
This is a double honour, Burgundy:
Yet heavens have glory for this victory!

BURGUNDY
Warlike and martial Talbot, Burgundy
Enshrines thee in his heart and there erects
Thy noble deeds as valour's monuments.

TALBOT
Thanks, gentle duke. But where is Pucelle now?
I think her old familiar is asleep:
Now where's the Bastard's braves, and Charles his gleeks?
What, all amort? Rouen hangs her head for grief
That such a valiant company are fled.
Now will we take some order in the town,
Placing therein some expert officers,
And then depart to Paris to the king,
For there young Henry with his nobles lie.

BURGUNDY
What wills Lord Talbot pleaseth Burgundy.

TALBOT
But yet, before we go, let's not forget
The noble Duke of Bedford late deceased,
But see his exequies fulfill'd in Rouen:
A braver soldier never couched lance,
A gentler heart did never sway in court;

But kings and mightiest potentates must die,
For that's the end of human misery.

Exeunt

Enter CHARLES, the BASTARD OF ORLEANS, ALENCON, JOAN LA PUCELLE, and forces

JOAN LA PUCELLE
Dismay not, princes, at this accident,
Nor grieve that Rouen is so recovered:
Care is no cure, but rather corrosive,
For things that are not to be remedied.
Let frantic Talbot triumph for a while
And like a peacock sweep along his tail;
We'll pull his plumes and take away his train,
If Dauphin and the rest will be but ruled.

CHARLES
We have been guided by thee hitherto,
And of thy cunning had no diffidence:
One sudden foil shall never breed distrust.

BASTARD OF ORLEANS
Search out thy wit for secret policies,
And we will make thee famous through the world.

ALENCON
We'll set thy statue in some holy place,
And have thee reverenced like a blessed saint:
Employ thee then, sweet virgin, for our good.

JOAN LA PUCELLE
Then thus it must be; this doth Joan devise:
By fair persuasions mix'd with sugar'd words
We will entice the Duke of Burgundy
To leave the Talbot and to follow us.

CHARLES
Ay, marry, sweeting, if we could do that,
France were no place for Henry's warriors;
Nor should that nation boast it so with us,
But be extirped from our provinces.

ALENCON
For ever should they be expulsed from France
And not have title of an earldom here.

JOAN LA PUCELLE
Your honours shall perceive how I will work
To bring this matter to the wished end.

Drum sounds afar off

Hark! by the sound of drum you may perceive
Their powers are marching unto Paris-ward.

Here sound an English march. Enter, and pass over at a distance, TALBOT and his forces

There goes the Talbot, with his colours spread,
And all the troops of English after him.

French march. Enter BURGUNDY and forces

Now in the rearward comes the duke and his:
Fortune in favour makes him lag behind.
Summon a parley; we will talk with him.

Trumpets sound a parley

CHARLES
A parley with the Duke of Burgundy!

BURGUNDY
Who craves a parley with the Burgundy?

JOAN LA PUCELLE
The princely Charles of France, thy countryman.

BURGUNDY
What say'st thou, Charles? for I am marching hence.

CHARLES
Speak, Pucelle, and enchant him with thy words.

JOAN LA PUCELLE
Brave Burgundy, undoubted hope of France!
Stay, let thy humble handmaid speak to thee.

BURGUNDY
Speak on; but be not over-tedious.

JOAN LA PUCELLE
Look on thy country, look on fertile France,
And see the cities and the towns defaced
By wasting ruin of the cruel foe.
As looks the mother on her lowly babe
When death doth close his tender dying eyes,
See, see the pining malady of France;

Behold the wounds, the most unnatural wounds,
Which thou thyself hast given her woful breast.
O, turn thy edged sword another way;
Strike those that hurt, and hurt not those that help.
One drop of blood drawn from thy country's bosom
Should grieve thee more than streams of foreign gore:
Return thee therefore with a flood of tears,
And wash away thy country's stained spots.

BURGUNDY
Either she hath bewitch'd me with her words,
Or nature makes me suddenly relent.

JOAN LA PUCELLE
Besides, all French and France exclaims on thee,
Doubting thy birth and lawful progeny.
Who joint'st thou with but with a lordly nation
That will not trust thee but for profit's sake?
When Talbot hath set footing once in France
And fashion'd thee that instrument of ill,
Who then but English Henry will be lord
And thou be thrust out like a fugitive?
Call we to mind, and mark but this for proof,
Was not the Duke of Orleans thy foe?
And was he not in England prisoner?
But when they heard he was thine enemy,
They set him free without his ransom paid,
In spite of Burgundy and all his friends.
See, then, thou fight'st against thy countrymen
And joint'st with them will be thy slaughtermen.
Come, come, return; return, thou wandering lord:
Charles and the rest will take thee in their arms.

BURGUNDY
I am vanquished; these haughty words of hers
Have batter'd me like roaring cannon-shot,
And made me almost yield upon my knees.
Forgive me, country, and sweet countrymen,
And, lords, accept this hearty kind embrace:
My forces and my power of men are yours:
So farewell, Talbot; I'll no longer trust thee.

JOAN LA PUCELLE
[Aside] Done like a Frenchman: turn, and turn again!

CHARLES
Welcome, brave duke! thy friendship makes us fresh.

BASTARD OF ORLEANS
And doth beget new courage in our breasts.

ALENCON
Pucelle hath bravely play'd her part in this,
And doth deserve a coronet of gold.

CHARLES
Now let us on, my lords, and join our powers,
And seek how we may prejudice the foe.

Exeunt

SCENE IV. Paris. The Palace.

Enter KING HENRY VI, GLOUCESTER, BISHOP OF WINCHESTER, YORK, SUFFOLK, SOMERSET,
WARWICK, EXETER, VERNON BASSET, and others. To them with his Soldiers, TALBOT

TALBOT
My gracious prince, and honourable peers,
Hearing of your arrival in this realm,
I have awhile given truce unto my wars,
To do my duty to my sovereign:
In sign, whereof, this arm, that hath reclaim'd
To your obedience fifty fortresses,
Twelve cities and seven walled towns of strength,
Beside five hundred prisoners of esteem,
Lets fall his sword before your highness' feet,
And with submissive loyalty of heart
Ascribes the glory of his conquest got
First to my God and next unto your grace.

Kneels

KING HENRY VI
Is this the Lord Talbot, uncle Gloucester,
That hath so long been resident in France?

GLOUCESTER
Yes, if it please your majesty, my liege.

KING HENRY VI
Welcome, brave captain and victorious lord!
When I was young, as yet I am not old,
I do remember how my father said
A stouter champion never handled sword.
Long since we were resolved of your truth,
Your faithful service and your toil in war;
Yet never have you tasted our reward,
Or been reguerdon'd with so much as thanks,
Because till now we never saw your face:
Therefore, stand up; and, for these good deserts,

We here create you Earl of Shrewsbury;
And in our coronation take your place.

Sennet.

Flourish.

Exeunt all but VERNON and BASSET

VERNON
Now, sir, to you, that were so hot at sea,
Disgracing of these colours that I wear
In honour of my noble Lord of York:
Darest thou maintain the former words thou spakest?

BASSET
Yes, sir; as well as you dare patronage
The envious barking of your saucy tongue
Against my lord the Duke of Somerset.

VERNON
Sirrah, thy lord I honour as he is.

BASSET
Why, what is he? as good a man as York.

VERNON
Hark ye; not so: in witness, take ye that.

Strikes him

BASSET
Villain, thou know'st the law of arms is such
That whoso draws a sword, 'tis present death,
Or else this blow should broach thy dearest blood.
But I'll unto his majesty, and crave
I may have liberty to venge this wrong;
When thou shalt see I'll meet thee to thy cost.

VERNON
Well, miscreant, I'll be there as soon as you;
And, after, meet you sooner than you would.

Exeunt

ACT IV

SCENE I. Paris. A Hall of State.

Enter KING HENRY VI, GLOUCESTER, BISHOP OF WINCHESTER, YORK, SUFFOLK, SOMERSET,
WARWICK, TALBOT, EXETER, the Governor, of Paris, and others

GLOUCESTER
Lord bishop, set the crown upon his head.

BISHOP OF WINCHESTER
God save King Henry, of that name the sixth!

GLOUCESTER
Now, governor of Paris, take your oath,
That you elect no other king but him;
Esteem none friends but such as are his friends,
And none your foes but such as shall pretend
Malicious practises against his state:
This shall ye do, so help you righteous God!

Enter FASTOLFE

FASTOLFE
My gracious sovereign, as I rode from Calais,
To haste unto your coronation,
A letter was deliver'd to my hands,
Writ to your grace from the Duke of Burgundy.

TALBOT
Shame to the Duke of Burgundy and thee!
I vow'd, base knight, when I did meet thee next,
To tear the garter from thy craven's leg,

Plucking it off

Which I have done, because unworthily
Thou wast installed in that high degree.
Pardon me, princely Henry, and the rest
This dastard, at the battle of Patay,
When but in all I was six thousand strong
And that the French were almost ten to one,
Before we met or that a stroke was given,
Like to a trusty squire did run away:
In which assault we lost twelve hundred men;
Myself and divers gentlemen beside
Were there surprised and taken prisoners.
Then judge, great lords, if I have done amiss;
Or whether that such cowards ought to wear
This ornament of knighthood, yea or no.

GLOUCESTER

To say the truth, this fact was infamous
And ill beseeming any common man,
Much more a knight, a captain and a leader.

TALBOT
When first this order was ordain'd, my lords,
Knights of the garter were of noble birth,
Valiant and virtuous, full of haughty courage,
Such as were grown to credit by the wars;
Not fearing death, nor shrinking for distress,
But always resolute in most extremes.
He then that is not furnish'd in this sort
Doth but usurp the sacred name of knight,
Profaning this most honourable order,
And should, if I were worthy to be judge,
Be quite degraded, like a hedge-born swain
That doth presume to boast of gentle blood.

KING HENRY VI
Stain to thy countrymen, thou hear'st thy doom!
Be packing, therefore, thou that wast a knight:
Henceforth we banish thee, on pain of death.

Exit FASTOLFE

And now, my lord protector, view the letter
Sent from our uncle Duke of Burgundy.

GLOUCESTER
What means his grace, that he hath changed his style?
No more but, plain and bluntly, 'To the king!'
Hath he forgot he is his sovereign?
Or doth this churlish superscription
Pretend some alteration in good will?
What's here?

Reads

'I have, upon especial cause,
Moved with compassion of my country's wreck,
Together with the pitiful complaints
Of such as your oppression feeds upon,
Forsaken your pernicious faction
And join'd with Charles, the rightful King of France.'
O monstrous treachery! can this be so,
That in alliance, amity and oaths,
There should be found such false dissembling guile?

KING HENRY VI
What! doth my uncle Burgundy revolt?

GLOUCESTER
He doth, my lord, and is become your foe.

KING HENRY VI
Is that the worst this letter doth contain?

GLOUCESTER
It is the worst, and all, my lord, he writes.

KING HENRY VI
Why, then, Lord Talbot there shall talk with him
And give him chastisement for this abuse.
How say you, my lord? are you not content?

TALBOT
Content, my liege! yes, but that I am prevented,
I should have begg'd I might have been employ'd.

KING HENRY VI
Then gather strength and march unto him straight:
Let him perceive how ill we brook his treason
And what offence it is to flout his friends.

TALBOT
I go, my lord, in heart desiring still
You may behold confusion of your foes.

Exit

Enter VERNON and BASSET

VERNON
Grant me the combat, gracious sovereign.

BASSET
And me, my lord, grant me the combat too.

YORK
This is my servant: hear him, noble prince.

SOMERSET
And this is mine: sweet Henry, favour him.

KING HENRY VI
Be patient, lords; and give them leave to speak.
Say, gentlemen, what makes you thus exclaim?
And wherefore crave you combat? or with whom?

VERNON
With him, my lord; for he hath done me wrong.

BASSET
And I with him; for he hath done me wrong.

KING HENRY VI
What is that wrong whereof you both complain?
First let me know, and then I'll answer you.

BASSET
Crossing the sea from England into France,
This fellow here, with envious carping tongue,
Upbraided me about the rose I wear;
Saying, the sanguine colour of the leaves
Did represent my master's blushing cheeks,
When stubbornly he did repugn the truth
About a certain question in the law
Argued betwixt the Duke of York and him;
With other vile and ignominious terms:
In confutation of which rude reproach
And in defence of my lord's worthiness,
I crave the benefit of law of arms.

VERNON
And that is my petition, noble lord:
For though he seem with forged quaint conceit
To set a gloss upon his bold intent,
Yet know, my lord, I was provoked by him;
And he first took exceptions at this badge,
Pronouncing that the paleness of this flower
Bewray'd the faintness of my master's heart.

YORK
Will not this malice, Somerset, be left?

SOMERSET
Your private grudge, my Lord of York, will out,
Though ne'er so cunningly you smother it.

KING HENRY VI
Good Lord, what madness rules in brainsick men,
When for so slight and frivolous a cause
Such factious emulations shall arise!
Good cousins both, of York and Somerset,
Quiet yourselves, I pray, and be at peace.

YORK
Let this dissension first be tried by fight,
And then your highness shall command a peace.

SOMERSET
The quarrel toucheth none but us alone;
Betwixt ourselves let us decide it then.

YORK
There is my pledge; accept it, Somerset.

VERNON
Nay, let it rest where it began at first.

BASSET
Confirm it so, mine honourable lord.

GLOUCESTER
Confirm it so! Confounded be your strife!
And perish ye, with your audacious prate!
Presumptuous vassals, are you not ashamed
With this immodest clamorous outrage
To trouble and disturb the king and us?
And you, my lords, methinks you do not well
To bear with their perverse objections;
Much less to take occasion from their mouths
To raise a mutiny betwixt yourselves:
Let me persuade you take a better course.

EXETER
It grieves his highness: good my lords, be friends.

KING HENRY VI
Come hither, you that would be combatants:
Henceforth I charge you, as you love our favour,
Quite to forget this quarrel and the cause.
And you, my lords, remember where we are,
In France, amongst a fickle wavering nation:
If they perceive dissension in our looks
And that within ourselves we disagree,
How will their grudging stomachs be provoked
To wilful disobedience, and rebel!
Beside, what infamy will there arise,
When foreign princes shall be certified
That for a toy, a thing of no regard,
King Henry's peers and chief nobility
Destroy'd themselves, and lost the realm of France!
O, think upon the conquest of my father,
My tender years, and let us not forego
That for a trifle that was bought with blood
Let me be umpire in this doubtful strife.
I see no reason, if I wear this rose,

Putting on a red rose

That any one should therefore be suspicious
I more incline to Somerset than York:
Both are my kinsmen, and I love them both:

As well they may upbraid me with my crown,
Because, forsooth, the king of Scots is crown'd.
But your discretions better can persuade
Than I am able to instruct or teach:
And therefore, as we hither came in peace,
So let us still continue peace and love.
Cousin of York, we institute your grace
To be our regent in these parts of France:
And, good my Lord of Somerset, unite
Your troops of horsemen with his bands of foot;
And, like true subjects, sons of your progenitors,
Go cheerfully together and digest.
Your angry choler on your enemies.
Ourself, my lord protector and the rest
After some respite will return to Calais;
From thence to England; where I hope ere long
To be presented, by your victories,
With Charles, Alencon and that traitorous rout.

Flourish.

Exeunt all but YORK, WARWICK, EXETER and VERNON

WARWICK
My Lord of York, I promise you, the king
Prettily, methought, did play the orator.

YORK
And so he did; but yet I like it not,
In that he wears the badge of Somerset.

WARWICK
Tush, that was but his fancy, blame him not;
I dare presume, sweet prince, he thought no harm.

YORK
An if I wist he did,--but let it rest;
Other affairs must now be managed.

Exeunt all but EXETER

EXETER
Well didst thou, Richard, to suppress thy voice;
For, had the passions of thy heart burst out,
I fear we should have seen decipher'd there
More rancorous spite, more furious raging broils,
Than yet can be imagined or supposed.
But howsoe'er, no simple man that sees
This jarring discord of nobility,
This shouldering of each other in the court,
This factious bandying of their favourites,

But that it doth presage some ill event.
'Tis much when sceptres are in children's hands;
But more when envy breeds unkind division;
There comes the rain, there begins confusion.

Exit

Enter TALBOT, with trump and drum

TALBOT
Go to the gates of Bourdeaux, trumpeter:
Summon their general unto the wall.

Trumpet sounds.

Enter GENERAL and others, aloft

English John Talbot, captains, calls you forth,
Servant in arms to Harry King of England;
And thus he would: Open your city gates;
Be humble to us; call my sovereign yours,
And do him homage as obedient subjects;
And I'll withdraw me and my bloody power:
But, if you frown upon this proffer'd peace,
You tempt the fury of my three attendants,
Lean famine, quartering steel, and climbing fire;
Who in a moment even with the earth
Shall lay your stately and air-braving towers,
It you forsake the offer of their love.

GENERAL
Thou ominous and fearful owl of death,
Our nation's terror and their bloody scourge!
The period of thy tyranny approacheth.
On us thou canst not enter but by death;
For, I protest, we are well fortified
And strong enough to issue out and fight:
If thou retire, the Dauphin, well appointed,
Stands with the snares of war to tangle thee:
On either hand thee there are squadrons pitch'd,
To wall thee from the liberty of flight;
And no way canst thou turn thee for redress,
But death doth front thee with apparent spoil
And pale destruction meets thee in the face.
Ten thousand French have ta'en the sacrament
To rive their dangerous artillery
Upon no Christian soul but English Talbot.

Lo, there thou stand'st, a breathing valiant man,
Of an invincible unconquer'd spirit!
This is the latest glory of thy praise
That I, thy enemy, due thee withal;
For ere the glass, that now begins to run,
Finish the process of his sandy hour,
These eyes, that see thee now well coloured,
Shall see thee wither'd, bloody, pale and dead.

Drum afar off

Hark! hark! the Dauphin's drum, a warning bell,
Sings heavy music to thy timorous soul;
And mine shall ring thy dire departure out.

Exeunt GENERAL, & c

TALBOT
He fables not; I hear the enemy:
Out, some light horsemen, and peruse their wings.
O, negligent and heedless discipline!
How are we park'd and bounded in a pale,
A little herd of England's timorous deer,
Mazed with a yelping kennel of French curs!
If we be English deer, be then in blood;
Not rascal-like, to fall down with a pinch,
But rather, moody-mad and desperate stags,
Turn on the bloody hounds with heads of steel
And make the cowards stand aloof at bay:
Sell every man his life as dear as mine,
And they shall find dear deer of us, my friends.
God and Saint George, Talbot and England's right,
Prosper our colours in this dangerous fight!

Exeunt

SCENE III. Plains in Gascony.

Enter a MESSENGER that meets YORK.

Enter YORK with trumpet and many Soldiers

YORK
Are not the speedy scouts return'd again,
That dogg'd the mighty army of the Dauphin?

MESSENGER
They are return'd, my lord, and give it out
That he is march'd to Bourdeaux with his power,

To fight with Talbot: as he march'd along,
By your espials were discovered
Two mightier troops than that the Dauphin led,
Which join'd with him and made their march for Bourdeaux.

YORK

A plague upon that villain Somerset,
That thus delays my promised supply
Of horsemen, that were levied for this siege!
Renowned Talbot doth expect my aid,
And I am lowted by a traitor villain
And cannot help the noble chevalier:
God comfort him in this necessity!
If he miscarry, farewell wars in France.

Enter Sir William LUCY

LUCY

Thou princely leader of our English strength,
Never so needful on the earth of France,
Spur to the rescue of the noble Talbot,
Who now is girdled with a waist of iron
And hemm'd about with grim destruction:
To Bourdeaux, warlike duke! to Bourdeaux, York!
Else, farewell Talbot, France, and England's honour.

YORK

O God, that Somerset, who in proud heart
Doth stop my cornets, were in Talbot's place!
So should we save a valiant gentleman
By forfeiting a traitor and a coward.
Mad ire and wrathful fury makes me weep,
That thus we die, while remiss traitors sleep.

LUCY

O, send some succor to the distress'd lord!

YORK

He dies, we lose; I break my warlike word;
We mourn, France smiles; we lose, they daily get;
All 'long of this vile traitor Somerset.

LUCY

Then God take mercy on brave Talbot's soul;
And on his son young John, who two hours since
I met in travel toward his warlike father!
This seven years did not Talbot see his son;
And now they meet where both their lives are done.

YORK

Alas, what joy shall noble Talbot have
To bid his young son welcome to his grave?
Away! vexation almost stops my breath,
That sunder'd friends greet in the hour of death.
Lucy, farewell; no more my fortune can,
But curse the cause I cannot aid the man.
Maine, Blois, Poictiers, and Tours, are won away,
'Long all of Somerset and his delay.

Exit, with his soldiers

LUCY
Thus, while the vulture of sedition
Feeds in the bosom of such great commanders,
Sleeping neglection doth betray to loss
The conquest of our scarce cold conqueror,
That ever living man of memory,
Henry the Fifth: whiles they each other cross,
Lives, honours, lands and all hurry to loss.

Exit

SCENE IV. Other Plains in Gascony.

Enter SOMERSET, with his army; a Captain of TALBOT's with him

SOMERSET
It is too late; I cannot send them now:
This expedition was by York and Talbot
Too rashly plotted: all our general force
Might with a sally of the very town
Be buckled with: the over-daring Talbot
Hath sullied all his gloss of former honour
By this unheedful, desperate, wild adventure:
York set him on to fight and die in shame,
That, Talbot dead, great York might bear the name.

CAPTAIN
Here is Sir William Lucy, who with me
Set from our o'ermatch'd forces forth for aid.

Enter Sir William LUCY

SOMERSET
How now, Sir William! whither were you sent?

LUCY
Whither, my lord? from bought and sold Lord Talbot;
Who, ring'd about with bold adversity,
Cries out for noble York and Somerset,

To beat assailing death from his weak legions:
And whiles the honourable captain there
Drops bloody sweat from his war-wearied limbs,
And, in advantage lingering, looks for rescue,
You, his false hopes, the trust of England's honour,
Keep off aloof with worthless emulation.
Let not your private discord keep away
The levied succors that should lend him aid,
While he, renowned noble gentleman,
Yields up his life unto a world of odds:
Orleans the Bastard, Charles, Burgundy,
Alencon, Reignier, compass him about,
And Talbot perisheth by your default.

SOMERSET
York set him on; York should have sent him aid.

LUCY
And York as fast upon your grace exclaims;
Swearing that you withhold his levied host,
Collected for this expedition.

SOMERSET
York lies; he might have sent and had the horse;
I owe him little duty, and less love;
And take foul scorn to fawn on him by sending.

LUCY
The fraud of England, not the force of France,
Hath now entrapp'd the noble-minded Talbot:
Never to England shall he bear his life;
But dies, betray'd to fortune by your strife.

SOMERSET
Come, go; I will dispatch the horsemen straight:
Within six hours they will be at his aid.

LUCY
Too late comes rescue: he is ta'en or slain;
For fly he could not, if he would have fled;
And fly would Talbot never, though he might.

SOMERSET
If he be dead, brave Talbot, then adieu!

LUCY
His fame lives in the world, his shame in you.

Exeunt

Enter TALBOT and JOHN his son

TALBOT
O young John Talbot! I did send for thee
To tutor thee in stratagems of war,
That Talbot's name might be in thee revived
When sapless age and weak unable limbs
Should bring thy father to his drooping chair.
But, O malignant and ill-boding stars!
Now thou art come unto a feast of death,
A terrible and unavoided danger:
Therefore, dear boy, mount on my swiftest horse;
And I'll direct thee how thou shalt escape
By sudden flight: come, dally not, be gone.

JOHN TALBOT
Is my name Talbot? and am I your son?
And shall I fly? O if you love my mother,
Dishonour not her honourable name,
To make a bastard and a slave of me!
The world will say, he is not Talbot's blood,
That basely fled when noble Talbot stood.

TALBOT
Fly, to revenge my death, if I be slain.

JOHN TALBOT
He that flies so will ne'er return again.

TALBOT
If we both stay, we both are sure to die.

JOHN TALBOT
Then let me stay; and, father, do you fly:
Your loss is great, so your regard should be;
My worth unknown, no loss is known in me.
Upon my death the French can little boast;
In yours they will, in you all hopes are lost.
Flight cannot stain the honour you have won;
But mine it will, that no exploit have done:
You fled for vantage, everyone will swear;
But, if I bow, they'll say it was for fear.
There is no hope that ever I will stay,
If the first hour I shrink and run away.
Here on my knee I beg mortality,
Rather than life preserved with infamy.

TALBOT

Shall all thy mother's hopes lie in one tomb?

JOHN TALBOT
Ay, rather than I'll shame my mother's womb.

TALBOT
Upon my blessing, I command thee go.

JOHN TALBOT
To fight I will, but not to fly the foe.

TALBOT
Part of thy father may be saved in thee.

JOHN TALBOT
No part of him but will be shame in me.

TALBOT
Thou never hadst renown, nor canst not lose it.

JOHN TALBOT
Yes, your renowned name: shall flight abuse it?

TALBOT
Thy father's charge shall clear thee from that stain.

JOHN TALBOT
You cannot witness for me, being slain.
If death be so apparent, then both fly.

TALBOT
And leave my followers here to fight and die?
My age was never tainted with such shame.

JOHN TALBOT
And shall my youth be guilty of such blame?
No more can I be sever'd from your side,
Than can yourself yourself in twain divide:
Stay, go, do what you will, the like do I;
For live I will not, if my father die.

TALBOT
Then here I take my leave of thee, fair son,
Born to eclipse thy life this afternoon.
Come, side by side together live and die.
And soul with soul from France to heaven fly.

Exeunt

SCENE VI. A Field of Battle.

Alarum: excursions, wherein JOHN TALBOT is hemmed about, and TALBOT rescues him

TALBOT
Saint George and victory! fight, soldiers, fight.
The regent hath with Talbot broke his word
And left us to the rage of France his sword.
Where is John Talbot? Pause, and take thy breath;
I gave thee life and rescued thee from death.

JOHN TALBOT
O, twice my father, twice am I thy son!
The life thou gavest me first was lost and done,
Till with thy warlike sword, despite of late,
To my determined time thou gavest new date.

TALBOT
When from the Dauphin's crest thy sword struck fire,
It warm'd thy father's heart with proud desire
Of bold-faced victory. Then leaden age,
Quicken'd with youthful spleen and warlike rage,
Beat down Alencon, Orleans, Burgundy,
And from the pride of Gallia rescued thee.
The ireful bastard Orleans, that drew blood
From thee, my boy, and had the maidenhood
Of thy first fight, I soon encountered,
And interchanging blows I quickly shed
Some of his bastard blood; and in disgrace
Bespoke him thus; 'Contaminated, base
And misbegotten blood I spill of thine,
Mean and right poor, for that pure blood of mine
Which thou didst force from Talbot, my brave boy:'
Here, purposing the Bastard to destroy,
Came in strong rescue. Speak, thy father's care,
Art thou not weary, John? how dost thou fare?
Wilt thou yet leave the battle, boy, and fly,
Now thou art seal'd the son of chivalry?
Fly, to revenge my death when I am dead:
The help of one stands me in little stead.
O, too much folly is it, well I wot,
To hazard all our lives in one small boat!
If I to-day die not with Frenchmen's rage,
To-morrow I shall die with mickle age:
By me they nothing gain an if I stay;
'Tis but the shortening of my life one day:
In thee thy mother dies, our household's name,
My death's revenge, thy youth, and England's fame:
All these and more we hazard by thy stay;
All these are saved if thou wilt fly away.

JOHN TALBOT

The sword of Orleans hath not made me smart;
These words of yours draw life-blood from my heart:
On that advantage, bought with such a shame.
To save a paltry life and slay bright fame,
Before young Talbot from old Talbot fly,
The coward horse that bears me fail and die!
And like me to the peasant boys of France,
To be shame's scorn and subject of mischance!
Surely, by all the glory you have won,
An if I fly, I am not Talbot's son:
Then talk no more of flight, it is no boot;
If son to Talbot, die at Talbot's foot.

TALBOT

Then follow thou thy desperate sire of Crete,
Thou Icarus; thy life to me is sweet:
If thou wilt fight, fight by thy father's side;
And, commendable proved, let's die in pride.

Exeunt

SCENE VII. Another Part of the Field.

Alarum: excursions.

Enter TALBOT led by a SERVANT

TALBOT

Where is my other life? mine own is gone;
O, where's young Talbot? where is valiant John?
Triumphant death, smear'd with captivity,
Young Talbot's valour makes me smile at thee:
When he perceived me shrink and on my knee,
His bloody sword he brandish'd over me,
And, like a hungry lion, did commence
Rough deeds of rage and stern impatience;
But when my angry guardant stood alone,
Tendering my ruin and assail'd of none,
Dizzy-eyed fury and great rage of heart
Suddenly made him from my side to start
Into the clustering battle of the French;
And in that sea of blood my boy did drench
His over-mounting spirit, and there died,
My Icarus, my blossom, in his pride.

SERVANT

O, my dear lord, lo, where your son is borne!

Enter Soldiers, with the body of JOHN TALBOT

TALBOT
Thou antic death, which laugh'st us here to scorn,
Anon, from thy insulting tyranny,
Coupled in bonds of perpetuity,
Two Talbots, winged through the lither sky,
In thy despite shall 'scape mortality.
O, thou, whose wounds become hard-favour'd death,
Speak to thy father ere thou yield thy breath!
Brave death by speaking, whether he will or no;
Imagine him a Frenchman and thy foe.
Poor boy! he smiles, methinks, as who should say,
Had death been French, then death had died to-day.
Come, come and lay him in his father's arms:
My spirit can no longer bear these harms.
Soldiers, adieu! I have what I would have,
Now my old arms are young John Talbot's grave.

Dies

Enter CHARLES, ALENCON, BURGUNDY, BASTARD OF ORLEANS, JOAN LA PUCELLE, and forces

CHARLES
Had York and Somerset brought rescue in,
We should have found a bloody day of this.

BASTARD OF ORLEANS
How the young whelp of Talbot's, raging-wood,
Did flesh his puny sword in Frenchmen's blood!

JOAN LA PUCELLE
Once I encounter'd him, and thus I said:
'Thou maiden youth, be vanquish'd by a maid:'
But, with a proud majestical high scorn,
He answer'd thus: 'Young Talbot was not born
To be the pillage of a giglot wench:'
So, rushing in the bowels of the French,
He left me proudly, as unworthy fight.

BURGUNDY
Doubtless he would have made a noble knight;
See, where he lies inhearsed in the arms
Of the most bloody nurser of his harms!

BASTARD OF ORLEANS
Hew them to pieces, hack their bones asunder
Whose life was England's glory, Gallia's wonder.

CHARLES

O, no, forbear! for that which we have fled
During the life, let us not wrong it dead.

Enter Sir William LUCY, attended; Herald of the French preceding

LUCY
Herald, conduct me to the Dauphin's tent,
To know who hath obtained the glory of the day.

CHARLES
On what submissive message art thou sent?

LUCY
Submission, Dauphin! 'tis a mere French word;
We English warriors wot not what it means.
I come to know what prisoners thou hast ta'en
And to survey the bodies of the dead.

CHARLES
For prisoners ask'st thou? hell our prison is.
But tell me whom thou seek'st.

LUCY
But where's the great Alcides of the field,
Valiant Lord Talbot, Earl of Shrewsbury,
Created, for his rare success in arms,
Great Earl of Washford, Waterford and Valence;
Lord Talbot of Goodrig and Urchinfield,
Lord Strange of Blackmere, Lord Verdun of Alton,
Lord Cromwell of Wingfield, Lord Furnival of Sheffield,
The thrice-victorious Lord of Falconbridge;
Knight of the noble order of Saint George,
Worthy Saint Michael and the Golden Fleece;
Great marshal to Henry the Sixth
Of all his wars within the realm of France?

JOAN LA PUCELLE
Here is a silly stately style indeed!
The Turk, that two and fifty kingdoms hath,
Writes not so tedious a style as this.
Him that thou magnifiest with all these titles
Stinking and fly-blown lies here at our feet.

LUCY
Is Talbot slain, the Frenchmen's only scourge,
Your kingdom's terror and black Nemesis?
O, were mine eyeballs into bullets turn'd,
That I in rage might shoot them at your faces!
O, that I could but call these dead to life!
It were enough to fright the realm of France:
Were but his picture left amongst you here,

It would amaze the proudest of you all.
Give me their bodies, that I may bear them hence
And give them burial as beseems their worth.

JOAN LA PUCELLE
I think this upstart is old Talbot's ghost,
He speaks with such a proud commanding spirit.
For God's sake let him have 'em; to keep them here,
They would but stink, and putrefy the air.

CHARLES
Go, take their bodies hence.

LUCY
I'll bear them hence; but from their ashes shall be rear'd
A phoenix that shall make all France afeard.

CHARLES
So we be rid of them, do with 'em what thou wilt.
And now to Paris, in this conquering vein:
All will be ours, now bloody Talbot's slain.

Exeunt

ACT V

SCENE I. London. The Palace.

Sennet.

Enter KING HENRY VI, GLOUCESTER, and EXETER

KING HENRY VI
Have you perused the letters from the pope,
The emperor and the Earl of Armagnac?

GLOUCESTER
I have, my lord: and their intent is this:
They humbly sue unto your excellence
To have a godly peace concluded of
Between the realms of England and of France.

KING HENRY VI
How doth your grace affect their motion?

GLOUCESTER

Well, my good lord; and as the only means
To stop effusion of our Christian blood
And 'stablish quietness on every side.

KING HENRY VI
Ay, marry, uncle; for I always thought
It was both impious and unnatural
That such immanity and bloody strife
Should reign among professors of one faith.

GLOUCESTER
Beside, my lord, the sooner to effect
And surer bind this knot of amity,
The Earl of Armagnac, near knit to Charles,
A man of great authority in France,
Proffers his only daughter to your grace
In marriage, with a large and sumptuous dowry.

KING HENRY VI
Marriage, uncle! alas, my years are young!
And fitter is my study and my books
Than wanton dalliance with a paramour.
Yet call the ambassador; and, as you please,
So let them have their answers every one:
I shall be well content with any choice
Tends to God's glory and my country's weal.

Enter CARDINAL OF WINCHESTER in Cardinal's habit, a Legate and two Ambassadors

EXETER
What! is my Lord of Winchester install'd,
And call'd unto a cardinal's degree?
Then I perceive that will be verified
Henry the Fifth did sometime prophesy,
'If once he come to be a cardinal,
He'll make his cap co-equal with the crown.'

KING HENRY VI
My lords ambassadors, your several suits
Have been consider'd and debated on.
And therefore are we certainly resolved
To draw conditions of a friendly peace;
Which by my Lord of Winchester we mean
Shall be transported presently to France.

GLOUCESTER
And for the proffer of my lord your master,
I have inform'd his highness so at large
As liking of the lady's virtuous gifts,
Her beauty and the value of her dower,
He doth intend she shall be England's queen.

KING HENRY VI
In argument and proof of which contract,
Bear her this jewel, pledge of my affection.
And so, my lord protector, see them guarded
And safely brought to Dover; where inshipp'd
Commit them to the fortune of the sea.

Exeunt all but CARDINAL OF WINCHESTER and LEGATE

CARDINAL OF WINCHESTER
Stay, my lord legate: you shall first receive
The sum of money which I promised
Should be deliver'd to his holiness
For clothing me in these grave ornaments.

LEGATE
I will attend upon your lordship's leisure.

CARDINAL OF WINCHESTER
[Aside] Now Winchester will not submit, I trow,
Or be inferior to the proudest peer.
Humphrey of Gloucester, thou shalt well perceive
That, neither in birth or for authority,
The bishop will be overborne by thee:
I'll either make thee stoop and bend thy knee,
Or sack this country with a mutiny.

Exeunt

SCENE II. France. Plains in Anjou.

Enter CHARLES, BURGUNDY, ALENCON, BASTARD OF ORLEANS, REIGNIER, JOAN LA PUCELLE, and forces

CHARLES
These news, my lord, may cheer our drooping spirits:
'Tis said the stout Parisians do revolt
And turn again unto the warlike French.

ALENCON
Then march to Paris, royal Charles of France,
And keep not back your powers in dalliance.

JOAN LA PUCELLE
Peace be amongst them, if they turn to us;
Else, ruin combat with their palaces!

Enter SCOUT

SCOUT
Success unto our valiant general,
And happiness to his accomplices!

CHARLES
What tidings send our scouts? I prithee, speak.

SCOUT
The English army, that divided was
Into two parties, is now conjoined in one,
And means to give you battle presently.

CHARLES
Somewhat too sudden, sirs, the warning is;
But we will presently provide for them.

BURGUNDY
I trust the ghost of Talbot is not there:
Now he is gone, my lord, you need not fear.

JOAN LA PUCELLE
Of all base passions, fear is most accursed.
Command the conquest, Charles, it shall be thine,
Let Henry fret and all the world repine.

CHARLES
Then on, my lords; and France be fortunate!

Exeunt

SCENE III. Before Angiers.

Alarum. Excursions.

Enter JOAN LA PUCELLE

JOAN LA PUCELLE
The regent conquers, and the Frenchmen fly.
Now help, ye charming spells and periapts;
And ye choice spirits that admonish me
And give me signs of future accidents.

Thunder

You speedy helpers, that are substitutes
Under the lordly monarch of the north,
Appear and aid me in this enterprise.

Enter Fiends

This speedy and quick appearance argues proof
Of your accustom'd diligence to me.
Now, ye familiar spirits, that are cull'd
Out of the powerful regions under earth,
Help me this once, that France may get the field.

They walk, and speak not

O, hold me not with silence over-long!
Where I was wont to feed you with my blood,
I'll lop a member off and give it you
In earnest of further benefit,
So you do condescend to help me now.

They hang their heads

No hope to have redress? My body shall
Pay recompense, if you will grant my suit.

They shake their heads

Cannot my body nor blood-sacrifice
Entreat you to your wonted furtherance?
Then take my soul, my body, soul and all,
Before that England give the French the foil.

They depart

See, they forsake me! Now the time is come
That France must vail her lofty-plumed crest
And let her head fall into England's lap.
My ancient incantations are too weak,
And hell too strong for me to buckle with:
Now, France, thy glory droopeth to the dust.

Exit
Excursions.

Re-enter JOAN LA PUCELLE fighting hand to hand with YORK. JOAN LA PUCELLE is taken. The French fly.

YORK
Damsel of France, I think I have you fast:
Unchain your spirits now with spelling charms
And try if they can gain your liberty.
A goodly prize, fit for the devil's grace!
See, how the ugly wench doth bend her brows,
As if with Circe she would change my shape!

JOAN LA PUCELLE
Changed to a worser shape thou canst not be.

YORK
O, Charles the Dauphin is a proper man;
No shape but his can please your dainty eye.

JOAN LA PUCELLE
A plaguing mischief light on Charles and thee!
And may ye both be suddenly surprised
By bloody hands, in sleeping on your beds!

YORK
Fell banning hag, enchantress, hold thy tongue!

JOAN LA PUCELLE
I prithee, give me leave to curse awhile.

YORK
Curse, miscreant, when thou comest to the stake.

Exeunt

Alarum.

Enter SUFFOLK with MARGARET in his hand

SUFFOLK
Be what thou wilt, thou art my prisoner.

Gazes on her

O fairest beauty, do not fear nor fly!
For I will touch thee but with reverent hands;
I kiss these fingers for eternal peace,
And lay them gently on thy tender side.
Who art thou? say, that I may honour thee.

MARGARET
Margaret my name, and daughter to a king,
The King of Naples, whosoe'er thou art.

SUFFOLK
An earl I am, and Suffolk am I call'd.
Be not offended, nature's miracle,
Thou art allotted to be ta'en by me:
So doth the swan her downy cygnets save,
Keeping them prisoner underneath her wings.
Yet, if this servile usage once offend.
Go, and be free again, as Suffolk's friend.

She is going

O, stay! I have no power to let her pass;
My hand would free her, but my heart says no
As plays the sun upon the glassy streams,
Twinkling another counterfeited beam,
So seems this gorgeous beauty to mine eyes.
Fain would I woo her, yet I dare not speak:
I'll call for pen and ink, and write my mind.
Fie, de la Pole! disable not thyself;
Hast not a tongue? is she not here?
Wilt thou be daunted at a woman's sight?
Ay, beauty's princely majesty is such,
Confounds the tongue and makes the senses rough.

MARGARET
Say, Earl of Suffolk--if thy name be so--
What ransom must I pay before I pass?
For I perceive I am thy prisoner.

SUFFOLK
How canst thou tell she will deny thy suit,
Before thou make a trial of her love?

MARGARET
Why speak'st thou not? what ransom must I pay?

SUFFOLK
She's beautiful, and therefore to be woo'd;
She is a woman, therefore to be won.

MARGARET
Wilt thou accept of ransom? yea, or no.

SUFFOLK
Fond man, remember that thou hast a wife;
Then how can Margaret be thy paramour?

MARGARET
I were best to leave him, for he will not hear.

SUFFOLK
There all is marr'd; there lies a cooling card.

MARGARET
He talks at random; sure, the man is mad.

SUFFOLK
And yet a dispensation may be had.

MARGARET

And yet I would that you would answer me.

SUFFOLK
I'll win this Lady Margaret. For whom?
Why, for my king: tush, that's a wooden thing!

MARGARET
He talks of wood: it is some carpenter.

SUFFOLK
Yet so my fancy may be satisfied,
And peace established between these realms
But there remains a scruple in that too;
For though her father be the King of Naples,
Duke of Anjou and Maine, yet is he poor,
And our nobility will scorn the match.

MARGARET
Hear ye, captain, are you not at leisure?

SUFFOLK
It shall be so, disdain they ne'er so much.
Henry is youthful and will quickly yield.
Madam, I have a secret to reveal.

MARGARET
What though I be enthrall'd? he seems a knight,
And will not any way dishonour me.

SUFFOLK
Lady, vouchsafe to listen what I say.

MARGARET
Perhaps I shall be rescued by the French;
And then I need not crave his courtesy.

SUFFOLK
Sweet madam, give me a hearing in a cause--
MARGARET
Tush, women have been captivate ere now.

SUFFOLK
Lady, wherefore talk you so?

MARGARET
I cry you mercy, 'tis but Quid for Quo.

SUFFOLK
Say, gentle princess, would you not suppose
Your bondage happy, to be made a queen?

MARGARET
To be a queen in bondage is more vile
Than is a slave in base servility;
For princes should be free.

SUFFOLK
And so shall you,
If happy England's royal king be free.

MARGARET
Why, what concerns his freedom unto me?

SUFFOLK
I'll undertake to make thee Henry's queen,
To put a golden sceptre in thy hand
And set a precious crown upon thy head,
If thou wilt condescend to be my—

MARGARET
What?

SUFFOLK
His love.

MARGARET
I am unworthy to be Henry's wife.

SUFFOLK
No, gentle madam; I unworthy am
To woo so fair a dame to be his wife,
And have no portion in the choice myself.
How say you, madam, are ye so content?

MARGARET
An if my father please, I am content.

SUFFOLK
Then call our captains and our colours forth.
And, madam, at your father's castle walls
We'll crave a parley, to confer with him.

A parley sounded.

Enter REIGNIER on the walls

See, Reignier, see, thy daughter prisoner!

REIGNIER
To whom?

SUFFOLK

To me.

REIGNIER
Suffolk, what remedy?
I am a soldier, and unapt to weep,
Or to exclaim on fortune's fickleness.

SU FFOLK
Yes, there is remedy enough, my lord:
Consent, and for thy honour give consent,
Thy daughter shall be wedded to my king;
Whom I with pain have woo'd and won thereto;
And this her easy-held imprisonment
Hath gained thy daughter princely liberty.

REIGNIER
Speaks Suffolk as he thinks?

SUFFOLK
Fair Margaret knows
That Suffolk doth not flatter, face, or feign.

REIGNIER
Upon thy princely warrant, I descend
To give thee answer of thy just demand.

Exit from the walls

SUFFOLK
And here I will expect thy coming.

Trumpets sound.

Enter REIGNIER, below

REIGNIER
Welcome, brave earl, into our territories:
Command in Anjou what your honour pleases.

SUFFOLK
Thanks, Reignier, happy for so sweet a child,
Fit to be made companion with a king:
What answer makes your grace unto my suit?

REIGNIER
Since thou dost deign to woo her little worth
To be the princely bride of such a lord;
Upon condition I may quietly
Enjoy mine own, the country Maine and Anjou,
Free from oppression or the stroke of war,
My daughter shall be Henry's, if he please.

SUFFOLK
That is her ransom; I deliver her;
And those two counties I will undertake
Your grace shall well and quietly enjoy.

REIGNIER
And I again, in Henry's royal name,
As deputy unto that gracious king,
Give thee her hand, for sign of plighted faith.

SUFFOLK
Reignier of France, I give thee kingly thanks,
Because this is in traffic of a king.

Aside

And yet, methinks, I could be well content
To be mine own attorney in this case.
I'll over then to England with this news,
And make this marriage to be solemnized.
So farewell, Reignier: set this diamond safe
In golden palaces, as it becomes.

REIGNIER
I do embrace thee, as I would embrace
The Christian prince, King Henry, were he here.

MARGARET
Farewell, my lord: good wishes, praise and prayers
Shall Suffolk ever have of Margaret.

Going

SUFFOLK
Farewell, sweet madam: but hark you, Margaret;
No princely commendations to my king?

MARGARET
Such commendations as becomes a maid,
A virgin and his servant, say to him.

SUFFOLK
Words sweetly placed and modestly directed.
But madam, I must trouble you again;
No loving token to his majesty?

MARGARET
Yes, my good lord, a pure unspotted heart,
Never yet taint with love, I send the king.

SUFFOLK
And this withal.

Kisses her

MARGARET
That for thyself: I will not so presume
To send such peevish tokens to a king.

Exeunt REIGNIER and MARGARET

SUFFOLK
O, wert thou for myself! But, Suffolk, stay;
Thou mayst not wander in that labyrinth;
There Minotaurs and ugly treasons lurk.
Solicit Henry with her wondrous praise:
Bethink thee on her virtues that surmount,
And natural graces that extinguish art;
Repeat their semblance often on the seas,
That, when thou comest to kneel at Henry's feet,
Thou mayst bereave him of his wits with wonder.

Exit

SCENE IV. Camp of the YORK in Anjou.

Enter YORK, WARWICK, and others

YORK
Bring forth that sorceress condemn'd to burn.

Enter JOAN LA PUCELLE, guarded, and a SHEPHERD

SHEPHERD
Ah, Joan, this kills thy father's heart outright!
Have I sought every country far and near,
And, now it is my chance to find thee out,
Must I behold thy timeless cruel death?
Ah, Joan, sweet daughter Joan, I'll die with thee!

JOAN LA PUCELLE
Decrepit miser! base ignoble wretch!
I am descended of a gentler blood:
Thou art no father nor no friend of mine.

SHEPHERD
Out, out! My lords, an please you, 'tis not so;
I did beget her, all the parish knows:

Her mother liveth yet, can testify
She was the first fruit of my bachelorship.

WARWICK
Graceless! wilt thou deny thy parentage?

YORK
This argues what her kind of life hath been,
Wicked and vile; and so her death concludes.

SHEPHERD
Fie, Joan, that thou wilt be so obstacle!
God knows thou art a collop of my flesh;
And for thy sake have I shed many a tear:
Deny me not, I prithee, gentle Joan.

JOAN LA PUCELLE
Peasant, avaunt! You have suborn'd this man,
Of purpose to obscure my noble birth.

SHEPHERD
'Tis true, I gave a noble to the priest
The morn that I was wedded to her mother.
Kneel down and take my blessing, good my girl.
Wilt thou not stoop? Now cursed be the time
Of thy nativity! I would the milk
Thy mother gave thee when thou suck'dst her breast,
Had been a little ratsbane for thy sake!
Or else, when thou didst keep my lambs a-field,
I wish some ravenous wolf had eaten thee!
Dost thou deny thy father, cursed drab?
O, burn her, burn her! hanging is too good.

Exit

YORK
Take her away; for she hath lived too long,
To fill the world with vicious qualities.

JOAN LA PUCELLE
First, let me tell you whom you have condemn'd:
Not me begotten of a shepherd swain,
But issued from the progeny of kings;
Virtuous and holy; chosen from above,
By inspiration of celestial grace,
To work exceeding miracles on earth.
I never had to do with wicked spirits:
But you, that are polluted with your lusts,
Stain'd with the guiltless blood of innocents,
Corrupt and tainted with a thousand vices,
Because you want the grace that others have,

You judge it straight a thing impossible
To compass wonders but by help of devils.
No, misconceived! Joan of Arc hath been
A virgin from her tender infancy,
Chaste and immaculate in very thought;
Whose maiden blood, thus rigorously effused,
Will cry for vengeance at the gates of heaven.

YORK
Ay, ay: away with her to execution!

WARWICK
And hark ye, sirs; because she is a maid,
Spare for no faggots, let there be enow:
Place barrels of pitch upon the fatal stake,
That so her torture may be shortened.

JOAN LA PUCELLE
Will nothing turn your unrelenting hearts?
Then, Joan, discover thine infirmity,
That warranteth by law to be thy privilege.
I am with child, ye bloody homicides:
Murder not then the fruit within my womb,
Although ye hale me to a violent death.

YORK
Now heaven forfend! the holy maid with child!

WARWICK
The greatest miracle that e'er ye wrought:
Is all your strict preciseness come to this?

YORK
She and the Dauphin have been juggling:
I did imagine what would be her refuge.

WARWICK
Well, go to; we'll have no bastards live;
Especially since Charles must father it.

JOAN LA PUCELLE
You are deceived; my child is none of his:
It was Alencon that enjoy'd my love.

YORK
Alencon! that notorious Machiavel!
It dies, an if it had a thousand lives.

JOAN LA PUCELLE

O, give me leave, I have deluded you:
'Twas neither Charles nor yet the duke I named,
But Reignier, king of Naples, that prevail'd.

WARWICK
A married man! that's most intolerable.

YORK
Why, here's a girl! I think she knows not well,
There were so many, whom she may accuse.

WARWICK
It's sign she hath been liberal and free.

YORK
And yet, forsooth, she is a virgin pure.
Strumpet, thy words condemn thy brat and thee:
Use no entreaty, for it is in vain.

JOAN LA PUCELLE
Then lead me hence; with whom I leave my curse:
May never glorious sun reflex his beams
Upon the country where you make abode;
But darkness and the gloomy shade of death
Environ you, till mischief and despair
Drive you to break your necks or hang yourselves!

Exit, guarded

YORK
Break thou in pieces and consume to ashes,
Thou foul accursed minister of hell!

Enter CARDINAL OF WINCHESTER, attended

CARDINAL OF WINCHESTER
Lord regent, I do greet your excellence
With letters of commission from the king.
For know, my lords, the states of Christendom,
Moved with remorse of these outrageous broils,
Have earnestly implored a general peace
Betwixt our nation and the aspiring French;
And here at hand the Dauphin and his train
Approacheth, to confer about some matter.

YORK
Is all our travail turn'd to this effect?
After the slaughter of so many peers,
So many captains, gentlemen and soldiers,
That in this quarrel have been overthrown
And sold their bodies for their country's benefit,

Shall we at last conclude effeminate peace?
Have we not lost most part of all the towns,
By treason, falsehood and by treachery,
Our great progenitors had conquered?
O Warwick, Warwick! I foresee with grief
The utter loss of all the realm of France.

WARWICK
Be patient, York: if we conclude a peace,
It shall be with such strict and severe covenants
As little shall the Frenchmen gain thereby.

Enter CHARLES, ALENCON, BASTARD OF ORLEANS, REIGNIER, and others

CHARLES
Since, lords of England, it is thus agreed
That peaceful truce shall be proclaim'd in France,
We come to be informed by yourselves
What the conditions of that league must be.

YORK
Speak, Winchester; for boiling choler chokes
The hollow passage of my poison'd voice,
By sight of these our baleful enemies.

CARDINAL OF WINCHESTER
Charles, and the rest, it is enacted thus:
That, in regard King Henry gives consent,
Of mere compassion and of lenity,
To ease your country of distressful war,
And suffer you to breathe in fruitful peace,
You shall become true liegemen to his crown:
And Charles, upon condition thou wilt swear
To pay him tribute, submit thyself,
Thou shalt be placed as viceroy under him,
And still enjoy thy regal dignity.

ALENCON
Must he be then as shadow of himself?
Adorn his temples with a coronet,
And yet, in substance and authority,
Retain but privilege of a private man?
This proffer is absurd and reasonless.

CHARLES
'Tis known already that I am possess'd
With more than half the Gallian territories,
And therein reverenced for their lawful king:
Shall I, for lucre of the rest unvanquish'd,
Detract so much from that prerogative,
As to be call'd but viceroy of the whole?

No, lord ambassador, I'll rather keep
That which I have than, coveting for more,
Be cast from possibility of all.

YORK
Insulting Charles! hast thou by secret means
Used intercession to obtain a league,
And, now the matter grows to compromise,
Stand'st thou aloof upon comparison?
Either accept the title thou usurp'st,
Of benefit proceeding from our king
And not of any challenge of desert,
Or we will plague thee with incessant wars.

REIGNIER
My lord, you do not well in obstinacy
To cavil in the course of this contract:
If once it be neglected, ten to one
We shall not find like opportunity.

ALENCON
To say the truth, it is your policy
To save your subjects from such massacre
And ruthless slaughters as are daily seen
By our proceeding in hostility;
And therefore take this compact of a truce,
Although you break it when your pleasure serves.

WARWICK
How say'st thou, Charles? shall our condition stand?

CHARLES
It shall;
Only reserved, you claim no interest
In any of our towns of garrison.

YORK
Then swear allegiance to his majesty,
As thou art knight, never to disobey
Nor be rebellious to the crown of England,
Thou, nor thy nobles, to the crown of England.
So, now dismiss your army when ye please:
Hang up your ensign, let your drums be still,
For here we entertain a solemn peace.

Exeunt

SCENE V. London. The Palace.

Enter SUFFOLK in conference with KING HENRY VI, GLOUCESTER and EXETER

KING HENRY VI
Your wondrous rare description, noble earl,
Of beauteous Margaret hath astonish'd me:
Her virtues graced with external gifts
Do breed love's settled passions in my heart:
And like as rigor of tempestuous gusts
Provokes the mightiest hulk against the tide,
So am I driven by breath of her renown
Either to suffer shipwreck or arrive
Where I may have fruition of her love.

SUFFOLK
Tush, my good lord, this superficial tale
Is but a preface of her worthy praise;
The chief perfections of that lovely dame
Had I sufficient skill to utter them,
Would make a volume of enticing lines,
Able to ravish any dull conceit:
And, which is more, she is not so divine,
So full-replete with choice of all delights,
But with as humble lowliness of mind
She is content to be at your command;
Command, I mean, of virtuous chaste intents,
To love and honour Henry as her lord.

KING HENRY VI
And otherwise will Henry ne'er presume.
Therefore, my lord protector, give consent
That Margaret may be England's royal queen.

GLOUCESTER
So should I give consent to flatter sin.
You know, my lord, your highness is betroth'd
Unto another lady of esteem:
How shall we then dispense with that contract,
And not deface your honour with reproach?

SUFFOLK
As doth a ruler with unlawful oaths;
Or one that, at a triumph having vow'd
To try his strength, forsaketh yet the lists
By reason of his adversary's odds:
A poor earl's daughter is unequal odds,
And therefore may be broke without offence.

GLOUCESTER
Why, what, I pray, is Margaret more than that?
Her father is no better than an earl,
Although in glorious titles he excel.

SUFFOLK
Yes, lord, her father is a king,
The King of Naples and Jerusalem;
And of such great authority in France
As his alliance will confirm our peace
And keep the Frenchmen in allegiance.

GLOUCESTER
And so the Earl of Armagnac may do,
Because he is near kinsman unto Charles.

EXETER
Beside, his wealth doth warrant a liberal dower,
Where Reignier sooner will receive than give.

SUFFOLK
A dower, my lords! disgrace not so your king,
That he should be so abject, base and poor,
To choose for wealth and not for perfect love.
Henry is able to enrich his queen
And not seek a queen to make him rich:
So worthless peasants bargain for their wives,
As market-men for oxen, sheep, or horse.
Marriage is a matter of more worth
Than to be dealt in by attorneyship;
Not whom we will, but whom his grace affects,
Must be companion of his nuptial bed:
And therefore, lords, since he affects her most,
It most of all these reasons bindeth us,
In our opinions she should be preferr'd.
For what is wedlock forced but a hell,
An age of discord and continual strife?
Whereas the contrary bringeth bliss,
And is a pattern of celestial peace.
Whom should we match with Henry, being a king,
But Margaret, that is daughter to a king?
Her peerless feature, joined with her birth,
Approves her fit for none but for a king:
Her valiant courage and undaunted spirit,
More than in women commonly is seen,
Will answer our hope in issue of a king;
For Henry, son unto a conqueror,
Is likely to beget more conquerors,
If with a lady of so high resolve
As is fair Margaret he be link'd in love.
Then yield, my lords; and here conclude with me
That Margaret shall be queen, and none but she.

KING HENRY VI

Whether it be through force of your report,
My noble Lord of Suffolk, or for that
My tender youth was never yet attaint
With any passion of inflaming love,
I cannot tell; but this I am assured,
I feel such sharp dissension in my breast,
Such fierce alarums both of hope and fear,
As I am sick with working of my thoughts.
Take, therefore, shipping; post, my lord, to France;
Agree to any covenants, and procure
That Lady Margaret do vouchsafe to come
To cross the seas to England and be crown'd
King Henry's faithful and anointed queen:
For your expenses and sufficient charge,
Among the people gather up a tenth.
Be gone, I say; for, till you do return,
I rest perplexed with a thousand cares.
And you, good uncle, banish all offence:
If you do censure me by what you were,
Not what you are, I know it will excuse
This sudden execution of my will.
And so, conduct me where, from company,
I may revolve and ruminate my grief.

Exit

GLOUCESTER
Ay, grief, I fear me, both at first and last.

Exeunt GLOUCESTER and EXETER

SUFFOLK
Thus Suffolk hath prevail'd; and thus he goes,
As did the youthful Paris once to Greece,
With hope to find the like event in love,
But prosper better than the Trojan did.
Margaret shall now be queen, and rule the king;
But I will rule both her, the king and realm.

Exit

William Shakespeare – A Short Biography

The life of William Shakespeare, arguably the most significant figure in the Western literary canon, is
relatively unknown. Even the exact date of his birth is uncertain. April 23rd, the date now generally
accepted to be the date of his birth, is a result of a scholarly mistake and the appealing coincidence
of its being also the day of his death.

That so little is known about a writer with such great literary scope and accomplishment has naturally invited speculation and conspiracy theories about the authenticity of his authorship, his influence and even his existence.

Shakespeare was born in Stratford-upon-Avon in 1565, possibly on the 23rd April, St. George's Day, and baptised there on 26th April. His father was John Shakespeare, a successful glover and alderman who hailed from Snitterfield. His mother was Mary Arden, whose father was an affluent landowner. In total their union bore eight children; William was the third of these and the eldest surviving son.

Although there is no hard evidence on his education it is widely agreed among scholars that William attended the King's New School in Stratford which was chartered as a free school in 1553. This school was only a quarter of a mile from the house in which he spent his childhood, but since there are no attendance records existing it is assumed, rather than known, this was the base for his education.

Although the quality of education in a grammar school at that time varied wildly the curriculum did not, a key aspect of which, by royal decree, was Latin, and it is undoubtable that the school will have delivered an intensive education in Latin grammar, drawing heavily on the work of the classical Latin authors. If Shakespeare did attend this school then it is very likely the starting point for the fascination with and extensive knowledge of the classical Latin authors which would inform and inspire so much of his work began.

Little more detail is known of William's childhood, or his early teenage years, until, at the age of 18, he married Anne Hathaway, who was 26 and from the nearby village of Shottery. Her father was a yeoman farmer, and their family home a small farmhouse in the village. In his will he left her £6 13s 4d, six pounds, thirteen shillings and fourpence, to be paid on her wedding day. On November 27th, 1582 the consistory court of the Diocese of Worcester issued a marriage licence, and on the 28th two of Hathaway's neighbours, Fulk Sandells and John Richardson, posted bonds which guaranteed that there were no lawful claims to impede the marriage along with a surety of £40 to act as a financial guarantee for the wedding.

The marriage was conducted in some haste since, unusually, the marriage banns were read only once instead of the more normal three times, a decision which would have been taken by the Worcester chancellor. This haste is no doubt due to the child Anne delivered their first child, Susanna, six months later. Susanna, was baptised on May 26th, 1583. Several scholars have voiced their opinion that the wedding was imposed on a reluctant Shakespeare by Hathaway's outraged parents, although, again, there is nothing to formally support the theory. It has been further argued that the circumstances surrounding the wedding, particularly those of the neighbourly assurances, indicate that Shakespeare was involved with two women at the time of his marriage. According to the theory proposed by the early twentieth century scholar Frank Harris, Shakespeare had already chosen to marry a woman named Anne Whateley. It was only once this proposed union became known that Hathaway's outraged family forced him to marry their daughter. Harris goes on to surmise that Shakespeare considered the affair entrapment, and that this led to his wholesale despising of her, a "loathing for his wife [which] was measureless" and which ultimately caused him to leave Stratford and her and make for the theatre. But equally other scholars such as John Aubrey have responded to this with evidence that Shakespeare returned to Stratford every year which, if true, would rather diminish Harris's claim that Hathaway had poisoned Stratford for Shakespeare.

Harris's theory aside, Shakespeare and Hathaway had two more children, twins Hamnet and Judith, baptised on February 2nd,1585. Hamnet, Shakespeare's only son, died during one of the frequent outbreaks of bubonic plague and was buried on the August 11th, 1596, at the age of only eleven.

Little is known of Shakespeare's life during the years following the birth of the twins until he appears mentioned in relation to the London theatres in 1592, apart from a fleeting mention in the complaints bill of a legal case which came before the Queen's Bench court at Westminster, dated Michaelmas Term 1588 and October 9th, 1589. Despite this period of time being referred to in scholarly circles as Shakespeare's "lost years", there are several stories, apocryphal in nature, which are attributed to Shakespeare. For example, there is a legend in Stratford that he fled the town in order to avoid prosecution for poaching deer on the estate of Thomas Lucy, a local squire. It is also supposed that Shakespeare went so far as to take revenge on Lucy, a politician whose Protestantism opposed Shakespeare's Catholic childhood, by writing the following lampooning ballad about him:

> A parliament member, a justice of peace,
> At home a poor scarecrow, at London an ass,
> If lousy is Lucy as some folks miscall it
> Then Lucy is lousy whatever befall it.

However amusing the ballad and legend may be in imagining the life of a young Shakespeare, youthfully mischievous and still developing the wit, sense of adventure and humour which would become integral aspects of his writing, there is simply no evidence either to support the theory or to suggest that Shakespeare penned the ballad. Alongside this are suggestions that he began his theatrical career while minding the horses of the patrons of the London theatres and that he spent some time as a schoolmaster employed by one Alexander Hoghton, a Catholic landowner in Lancashire, in whose will is named "William Shakeshafte". However, this was a popular name in the Lancashire area at that time and there is no evidence that this referred to Shakespeare. The wealth of his writing makes it a frustrating exercise to learn more of his life and the manner in which he achieved those outstanding and lionized works.

Interestingly, the reference to Shakespeare in 1592 which ends the "lost years" is a piece of theatrical criticism by playwright Robert Greene in *Groats-Worth of Wit*. In a scathing passage Greene writes "...there is an upstart Crow, beautified with our feathers, that with his *Tiger's heart wrapped in a Player's hide*, supposes he is as well able to bombast out a blank verse as the best of you: and being an absolute *Johannes factotum*, is in his own conceit the only Shake-scene in a country." From this entry we can make some important inferences which shed light on Shakespeare's career, the first of which is that to be acknowledged, even negatively, by a playwright such as Robert Greene, by this point he must have been making significant impact on the London stage as a writer. Also of significance is the very meaning of the words themselves, for it is generally acknowledged that Shakespeare is being accused of writing with a lofty ambition beyond his capabilities and, more importantly, the capabilities of his contemporaries who were educated at Oxford and Cambridge. Within this remark, then, is an inherent snobbery which Shakespeare would come to resent and ultimately challenge in his writing. Though Greene's parody of "Oh, tiger's heart wrapped in a woman's hide" makes reference to *Henry VI, Part 3*, it is likely that Greene's opinion of Shakespeare was in part informed by another of Shakespeare's plays which was heavily criticised, *Titus Adronicus*, believed to have been written between 1588 and 1593. It was his first attempt at tragedy, almost prototypical, and was written at a time when, according to the scholar Jonathan Bate, he was "experimenting with ways of writing about and representing rape and seduction". Drawing heavily on the sixth book of Ovid's *Metamorphoses* as its main source of inspiration for the rape and mutilation of Lavinia, it offended the sensibilities of the more highbrow members of its audience, whilst presumably also simultaneously intimidating them with its detailed knowledge of

Ovid, a writer typically considered the reserve of the university-educated. Not only, then, was Shakespeare demonstrating a knowledge of classical literature which they thought befitted only a traditional scholar and thereby shining a light to the snobbery and exclusivity of such an education, but he was doing it radically and brilliantly.

By 1594 the Lord Chamberlain's Men had recognised his worthiness as a playwright and were performing his works. With the advantage of Shakespeare's progressive writing they rapidly became London's leading company of players, affording him more exposure and, following the death of Queen Elizabeth in 1603, a royal patent by the new king, James I, at which point they changed their name to the King's Men.

Before this success, though, several company members had formed a partnership to build their own theatre which came to be on the south bank of the river Thames, the now-famous and reconstructed Globe theatre. Though it is unclear precisely what Shakespeare's involvement in this venture was, records of his property and investments indicate that he came to be rich during this period, buying the second-largest house in Stratford, called New Place, in 1597, which he made his family home. Prior to this he was living in the parish of St Helen's Bishopsgate, north of the River Thames. He continued to spend most of his time at work in London and from about 1598-1602, he seems to have lived in the Paris Gardens area of Bankside south of the river near The Globe.

Despite efforts to pirate his work, Shakespeare's name was by 1598 so well known that it had already become a selling point in its own right on title pages.

An interesting aside is that theatres were mostly constructed on the south bank of the Thames (then part of the county of Surrey) as performing in London itself was thought to be a bad influence on the masses and subject to periodic bouts of censorship, repression and closing of venues which in the City itself was mainly courtyards and open areas at the many Inns.

Excluded from the City purpose built theatres began to be constructed outside the City limits. This area of the Thames though was rough and naturally vibrant with all sorts of characters, many of them of dubious nature or even criminal. It was also prone, due to its over-crowding and bad sanitation, to bouts of bubonic plague and other diseases particularly during the summer which was a further reason for the theatres there being closed. The Curtain, The Rose, The Swan, The Fortune, The Blackfriars and of course The Globe were all purpose built and situated here, some with an audience capacity approaching 3,000.

The first known printed copies of Shakespeare's plays date from 1594 in quarto editions, though these quarto editions are often considered "bad", a term referring to the likelihood of specific quarto editions being based on, for example, a reconstruction of a play as it was witnessed, rather than Shakespeare's original manuscript. The best example of such memorial reconstruction can be found in the differences between the first and second quarto editions of *Hamlet*. In examining Hamlet's most famous soliloquy, "to be or not to be", we can immediately recognise significant differences. First, the familiar second quarto version:

> To be, or not to be; that is the question:
> Whether 'tis nobler in the mind to suffer
> The slings and arrows of outrageous fortune,
> Or to take arms against a sea of troubles,
> And, by opposing, end them.

And, by contrast, the first quarto version:

> To be, or not to be, I there's the point,
> To Die, to sleep, is that all? I all:

For scholar Henry David Gray the first quarto lines are emblematic of "a distorted version of the completed drama filled out and revised by an inferior poet" and based, he goes on to argue, on the fractured memories of the play as witnessed and performed by the actor playing Marcellus. Gray, and several other critics, consider the first quarto a pirated copy, printed in haste without the writer's permission in an attempt to make quick money following the success of the play in the theatre. In understanding the significance of Marcellus to the theory it is imperative to note that the authenticity of each quarto is based on its similarities to the version of the play found in the first folio, printed in 1623 and believed to be authorised by Shakespeare. Therefore, since in the folio version of *Hamlet* the "to be or not to be" soliloquy is virtually identical to that of the second quarto, it is believed that the second was authored by Shakespeare himself and that the first, by its considerable differences, must therefore be in some way compromised. However, when read in comparison to the folio version, the only character whose lines are almost entirely perfect are those spoken by Marcellus, which, since dramatic practice at the time was for actors to be given only their own lines and three or four word 'cues' based on the lines preceding theirs, suggests that the first quarto is a memorial reconstruction of the play written by the actor who played Marcellus. Having committed his own lines to memory he was able to reproduce them accurately, but was left to fill in the remaining lines and plot from memory which accounts for the truncated and often vastly inferior writing in the first quarto.

According to the remaining cast lists from the period, Shakespeare remained an actor throughout his career as a writer, and it is thought he continued to act after he retired his pen. In 1616 he is recorded in the cast list in Ben Jonson's collected *Works* in the plays *Man in His Humour* 1598) and *Sejanus His Fall* (1603), though some scholars consider his absence from the list of Jonson's *Volpone* evidence that, by 1605, his acting career was nearing its end. Despite this in the First Folio he is listed as one of "the Principle Actors in all these Plays", several of which were only staged after *Volpone*.

By 1604 he had moved again, remaining north of the river, to an area near St. Paul's Cathedral where he rented a fine room amongst fine houses from Christopher Mountjoy, a French hatmaker and Huguenot.

The Anglo-Welsh poet John Davies of Hereford wrote in 1610 that "good Will" tended to play "kingly" roles, suggesting he was still on stage, perhaps now performing the more mature kings such as Lear and Henry VI. There has even been the suggestion that Shakespeare played the ghost of Hamlet's father, though there is little evidence to suggest it.

In 1608 the King's Men purchased the Blackfriars theatre from Henry Evans, and according to Cuthbert Burbage, one of the most highly regarded actors of the time, "placed many players" there "which were Heminges, Condell, Shakespeare, etc." A 1609 lawsuit brought against John Addenbrooke in Stratford on the 7th of June describes Shakespeare as "generosus nuper in curia domini Jacobi" (a gentleman recently at the court of King James) which indicates that by this time he was spending more time in Stratford. A likely cause of this was the bubonic plague, frequent outbreaks of which demanded the equally frequent closing of places of public gathering, principle among which were the theatres. Between May 1603 and February 1610 the theatres were closed for a total of 60 months, meaning there was no acting work and nobody to perform new plays. Though in 1610 Shakespeare returned to Stratford and it is supposed lived with his wife, he made frequent visits to London between 1611-14, being called as a witness in the trial *Bellott v. Mountjoy*, a case addressing concerns about the marriage settlement of Mountjoy's daughter, Mary. In March 1613 he purchased a gatehouse in the former Blackfriars priory, and spent several weeks in the city with his son-in-law John Hall, a physician, married to his daughter Susanna, from November 1614.

No plays are attributed to Shakespeare after 1613, and the last few plays he wrote before this time were in collaboration with other writers, one of whom is likely to be John Fletcher who succeeded him as the house playwright for the King's Men.

In early 1616 his daughter Judith married Thomas Quiney, a vintner and tobacconist. He signed his last will and testament on March 25th, of the same year, and the following day Quiney was ordered to do public penance for having fathered an illegitimate child with a woman named Margaret Wheeler who had died during childbirth which had enabled Quiney to cover up the scandal. This public humiliation would have been embarrassing for Shakespeare and his family.

William Shakespeare died two months later on April 23rd, 1616, survived by his wife and two daughters.

According to his will the bulk of his considerable estate was left to his elder daughter Susanna, with the instruction that she pass it down intact to "the first son of her body". However, though Susanna and Judith had four children between them they all died without progeny, ending Shakespeare's direct lineage. Also in his will was the instruction that his "second best bed" be left to his wife Anne, likely an insult, though the bed was possibly matrimonial and therefore of significant sentimental value.

He was buried two days after his death in the chancel of the Holy Trinity Church in Stratford-Upon-Avon.

The epitaph on the slab which covers his grave includes the following passage,

> Good frend for Iesvs sake forbeare,
> To digg the dvst encloased heare.
> Bleste be ye man yt spares thes stones,
> And cvrst be he yt moves my bones

which, in modern translation, reads

> Good friend, for Jesus's sake forbear,
> To dig the dust enclosed here.
> Blessed be the man that spares these stones,
> And cursed be he that moves my bones.

At some point before 1623 there was a funerary monument erected in his memory on the north wall of Stratford-upon-Avon which features a half-effigy of him writing, and which likens him to Nestor, Socrates and Virgil.

On January 29th, 1741 a white marble memorial statue to him was erected in Poets' Corner in Westminster Abbey.

Though there have been many monuments built around the world in memory of Shakespeare, undoubtedly the greatest memorial of all is the body of work which became the foundation of Western literary canon and an inspiration for every generation.

1589	Comedy of Errors (Comedy)
1590	Henry VI, Part II (History)
	Henry VI, Part III (History)
1591	Henry VI, Part I (History)
1592	Richard III (History)
1593	Taming of the Shrew (Comedy)
	Titus Andronicus (Tragedy)
	Venus and Adonis (Poem)
1594	Rape of Lucrece (Poem)
	Romeo and Juliet (Tragedy)
	Two Gentlemen of Verona (Comedy)
	Love's Labour's Lost (Comedy)
1595	Richard II (History)
	Midsummer Night's Dream (Comedy)
1596	King John (History)
	Merchant of Venice (Comedy)
1597	Henry IV, Part I (History)
	Henry IV, Part II (History)
1598	Passionate Pilgrim (Poem)
	Henry V (History)
	Much Ado about Nothing (Comedy)
1599	Twelfth Night (Comedy)
	As You Like It (Comedy)
	Julius Caesar (Tragedy)
1600	Hamlet (Tragedy)
	Merry Wives of Windsor (Comedy)
1601	Troilus and Cressida (Comedy)
1601	Phoenix and the Turtle (Poem))
1602	All's Well That Ends Well (Comedy)
1604	Othello (Tragedy)
	Measure for Measure

1605	King Lear (Tragedy)
	Macbeth (Tragedy)
1606	Antony and Cleopatra (Tragedy)
1607	Coriolanus (Tragedy)
	Timon of Athens (Tragedy)
1608	Pericles (Comedy)
1609	Cymbeline (Comedy)
	Lover's Complaint (Poem)
1610	Winter's Tale (Comedy)
1611	Tempest (Comedy)
1612	Henry VIII (History)

As regards his 154 sonnets it is almost impossible to date each individually though collectively they were first published in 1609, with two having been published in 1599.

Shakspeare; or, the Poet by Ralph Waldo Emerson

Great (1) men are more distinguished by range and extent than by originality. If we require the originality which consists in weaving, like a spider, their web from their own bowels; in finding clay and making bricks and building the house; no great men are original. Nor does valuable originality consist in unlikeness to other men. The hero is in the press of knights and the thick of events; and seeing what men want and sharing their desire, he adds the needful length of sight and of arm, to come at the desired point. The greatest genius is the most indebted man. A poet is no rattle-brain, saying what comes uppermost, and, because he says every thing, saying at last something good; but a heart in unison with his time and country. There is nothing whimsical and fantastic in his production, but sweet and sad earnest, freighted with the weightiest convictions and pointed with the most determined aim which any man or class knows of in his times. (2)

The Genius of our life is jealous of individuals, and will not have any individual great, except through the general. There is no choice to genius. A great man does not wake up on some fine morning and say, 'I am full of life, I will go to sea and find an Antarctic continent: to-day I will square the circle: I will ransack botany and find a new food for man: I have a new architecture in my mind: I foresee a new mechanic power:' no, but he finds himself in the river of the thoughts and events, forced onward by the ideas and necessities of his contemporaries. (3) He stands where all the eyes of men look one way, and their hands all point in the direction in which he should go. The Church has reared him amidst rites and pomps, and he carries out the advice which her music gave him, and builds a cathedral needed by her chants and processions. He finds a war raging: it educates him, by trumpet, in barracks, and he betters the instruction. He finds two counties groping to bring coal, or flour, or fish, from the place of production to the place of consumption, and he hits on a railroad. Every master has found his materials collected, and his power lay in his sympathy with his people and in his love of the materials he wrought in. What an economy of power! and what a compensation for the shortness of life! All is done to his hand. The world has brought him thus far on his way. The human race has gone out before him, sunk the hills, filled the hollows and bridged the rivers. Men, nations, poets, artisans, women, all have worked for him, and he enters into their labors. Choose any other thing, out of the line of tendency, out of the national feeling and history, and he would have all to do for himself: his powers would be expended in the first preparations. Great genial power, one would almost say, consists in not being original at all; in being altogether receptive; in letting the world do all, and suffering the spirit of the hour to pass unobstructed through the mind. (4)

Shakspeare's youth fell in a time when the English people were importunate for dramatic entertainments. The court took offence easily at political allusions and attempted to suppress them. The Puritans, a growing and energetic party, and the religious among the Anglican church, would suppress them. But the people wanted them. Inn-yards, houses without roofs, and extemporaneous enclosures at country fairs were the ready theatres of strolling players. The people had tasted this new joy; and, as we could not hope to suppress newspapers now,—no, not by the strongest party,— neither then could king, prelate, or puritan, alone or united, suppress an organ which was ballad, epic, newspaper, caucus, lecture, Punch and library, at the same time. Probably king, prelate and puritan, all found their own account in it. It had become, by all causes, a national interest,—by no means conspicuous, so that some great scholar would have thought of treating it in an English history,—but not a whit less considerable because it was cheap and of no account, like a baker's-shop. The best proof of its vitality is the crowd of writers which suddenly broke into this field; Kyd, Marlow, Greene, Jonson, Chapman, Dekker, Webster, Heywood, Middleton, Peele, Ford, Massinger, Beaumont and Fletcher.

The secure possession, by the stage, of the public mind, is of the first importance to the poet who works for it. (5) He loses no time in idle experiments. Here is audience and expectation prepared. In the case of Shakspeare there is much more. At the time when he left Stratford and went up to London, a great body of stage-plays of all dates and writers existed in manuscript and were in turn produced on the boards. Here is the Tale of Troy, which the audience will bear hearing some part of, every week; the Death of Julius Cæsar, and other stories out of Plutarch, which they never tire of; a shelf full of English history, from the chronicles of Brut and Arthur, down to the royal Henries, which men hear eagerly; and a string of doleful tragedies, merry Italian tales and Spanish voyages, which all the London 'prentices know. All the mass has been treated, with more or less skill, by every playwright, and the prompter has the soiled and tattered manuscripts. It is now no longer possible to say who wrote them first. They have been the property of the Theatre so long, and so many rising geniuses have enlarged or altered them, inserting a speech or a whole scene, or adding a song, that no man can any longer claim copyright in this work of numbers. Happily, no man wishes to. They are not yet desired in that way. We have few readers, many spectators and hearers. They had best lie where they are.

Shakspeare, in common with his comrades, esteemed the mass of old plays waste stock, in which any experiment could be freely tried. Had the prestige which hedges about a modern tragedy existed, nothing could have been done. The rude warm blood of the living England circulated in the play, as in street-ballads, and gave body which he wanted to his airy and majestic fancy. The poet needs a ground in popular tradition on which he may work, and which, again, may restrain his art within the due temperance. It holds him to the people, supplies a foundation for his edifice, and in furnishing so much work done to his hand, leaves him at leisure and in full strength for the audacities of his imagination. In short, the poet owes to his legend what sculpture owed to the temple. Sculpture in Egypt and in Greece grew up in subordination to architecture. It was the ornament of the temple wall: at first a rude relief carved on pediments, then the relief became bolder and a head or arm was projected from the wall; the groups being still arranged with reference to the building, which serves also as a frame to hold the figures; and when at last the greatest freedom of style and treatment was reached, the prevailing genius of architecture still enforced a certain calmness and continence in the statue. As soon as the statue was begun for itself, and with no reference to the temple or palace, the art began to decline: freak, extravagance and exhibition took the place of the old temperance. This balance-wheel, which the sculptor found in architecture, the perilous irritability of poetic talent found in the accumulated dramatic materials to which the people were already wonted, and which had a certain excellence which no single genius, however extraordinary, could hope to create.

In point of fact it appears that Shakspeare did owe debts in all directions, and was able to use whatever he found; and the amount of indebtedness may be inferred from Malone's laborious computations in regard to the First, Second and Third parts of Henry VI., in which, "out of 6043 lines, 1771 were written by some author preceding Shakspeare, 2373 by him, on the foundation laid by his predecessors, and 1899 were entirely his own." And the proceeding investigation hardly leaves a single drama of his absolute invention. Malone's sentence is an important piece of external history. In Henry VIII. I think I see plainly the cropping out of the original rock on which his own finer stratum was laid. The first play was written by a superior, thoughtful man, with a vicious ear. I can mark his lines, and know well their cadence. See Wolsey's soliloquy, and the following scene with Cromwell, where instead of the metre of Shakspeare, whose secret is that the thought constructs the tune, so that reading for the sense will best bring out the rhythm,—here the lines are constructed on a given tune, and the verse has even a trace of pulpit eloquence. But the play contains through all its length unmistakable traits of Shakspeare's hand, and some passages, as the account of the coronation, are like autographs. What is odd, the compliment to Queen Elizabeth is in the bad rhythm. (6)

Shakspeare knew that tradition supplies a better fable than any invention can. If he lost any credit of design, he augmented his resources; and, at that day, our petulant demand for originality was not so much pressed. There was no literature for the million. The universal reading, the cheap press, were unknown. A great poet who appears in illiterate times, absorbs into his sphere all the light which is any where radiating. Every intellectual jewel, every flower of sentiment it is his fine office to bring to his people; and he comes to value his memory equally with his invention. (7) He is therefore little solicitous whence his thoughts have been derived; whether through translation, whether through tradition, whether by travel in distant countries, whether by inspiration; from whatever source, they are equally welcome to his uncritical audience. Nay, he borrows very near home. Other men say wise things as well as he; only they say a good many foolish things, and do not know when they have spoken wisely. He knows the sparkle of the true stone, and puts it in high place, wherever he finds it. (8) Such is the happy position of Homer perhaps; of Chaucer, of Saadi. They felt that all wit was their wit. And they are librarians and historiographers, as well as poets. Each romancer was heir and dispenser of all the hundred tales of the world,—

"Presenting Thebes' and Pelops' line
And the tale of Troy divine." (9)

The influence of Chaucer is conspicuous in all our early literature; and more recently not only Pope and Dryden have been beholden to him, but, in the whole society of English writers, a large unacknowledged debt is easily traced. One is charmed with the opulence which feeds so many pensioners. But Chaucer is a huge borrower. Chaucer, it seems, drew continually, through Lydgate and Caxton, from Guido di Colonna, whose Latin romance of the Trojan war was in turn a compilation from Dares Phrygius, Ovid and Statius. Then Petrarch, Boccaccio and the Provençal poets are his benefactors: the Romaunt of the Rose is only judicious translation from William of Lorris and John of Meung: Troilus and Creseide, from Lollius of Urbino: The Cock and the Fox, from the Lais of Marie: The House of Fame, from the French or Italian: and poor Gower he uses as if he were only a brick-kiln or stone-quarry out of which to build his house. (10) He steals by this apology,—that what he takes has no worth where he finds it and the greatest where he leaves it. It has come to be practically a sort of rule in literature, that a man having once shown himself capable of original writing, is entitled thenceforth to steal from the writings of others at discretion. Thought is the property of him who can entertain it and of him who can adequately place it. A certain awkwardness marks the use of borrowed thoughts; but as soon as we have learned what to do with them they become our own.

Thus all originality is relative. Every thinker is retrospective. The learned member of the legislature, at Westminster or at Washington, speaks and votes for thousands. Show us the constituency, and the now invisible channels by which the senator is made aware of their wishes; the crowd of practical and knowing men, who, by correspondence or conversation, are feeding him with evidence, anecdotes and estimates, and it will bereave his fine attitude and resistance of something of their impressiveness. As Sir Robert Peel and Mr. Webster vote, so Locke and Rousseau think, for thousands; and so there were fountains all around Homer, (11) Menu, Saadi, or Milton, from which they drew; friends, lovers, books, traditions, proverbs,—all perished—which, if seen, would go to reduce the wonder. Did the bard speak with authority? Did he feel himself overmatched by any companion? The appeal is to the consciousness of the writer. Is there at last in his breast a Delphi whereof to ask concerning any thought or thing, whether it be verily so, yea or nay? and to have answer, and to rely on that? All the debts which such a man could contract to other wit would never disturb his consciousness of originality; for the ministrations of books and of other minds are a whiff of smoke to that most private reality with which he has conversed. (12)

It is easy to see that what is best written or done by genius in the world, was no man's work, but came by wide social labor, when a thousand wrought like one, sharing the same impulse. Our English Bible is a wonderful specimen of the strength and music of the English language. But it was not made by one man, or at one time; but centuries and churches brought it to perfection. There never was a time when there was not some translation existing. The Liturgy, admired for its energy and pathos, is an anthology of the piety of ages and nations, a translation of the prayers and forms of the Catholic church,—these collected, too, in long periods, from the prayers and meditations of every saint and sacred writer all over the world. (13) Grotius makes the like remark in respect to the Lord's Prayer, that the single clauses of which it is composed were already in use in the time of Christ, in the Rabbinical forms. He picked out the grains of gold. The nervous language of the Common Law, the impressive forms of our courts and the precision and substantial truth of the legal distinctions, are the contribution of all the sharp-sighted, strong-minded men who have lived in the countries where these laws govern. The translation of Plutarch gets its excellence by being translation on translation. There never was a time when there was none. All the truly idiomatic and national phrases are kept, and all others successively picked out and thrown away. Something like the same process had gone on, long before, with the originals of these books. The world takes liberties with world-books. Vedas, Æsop's Fables, Pilpay, Arabian Nights, Cid, Iliad, Robin Hood, Scottish Minstrelsy, are not the work of single men. In the composition of such works the time thinks, the market thinks, the mason, the carpenter, the merchant, the farmer, the fop, all think for us. Every book supplies its time with one good word; every municipal law, every trade, every folly of the day; and the generic catholic genius who is not afraid or ashamed to owe his originality to the originality of all, stands with the next age as the recorder and embodiment of his own. (14)

We have to thank the researches of antiquaries, and the Shakspeare Society, for ascertaining the steps of the English drama, from the Mysteries celebrated in churches and by churchmen, and the final detachment from the church, and the completion of secular plays, from Ferrex and Porrex, (15) and Gammer Gurton's Needle, down to the possession of the stage by the very pieces which Shakspeare altered, remodelled and finally made his own. Elated with success and piqued by the growing interest of the problem, they have left no bookstall unsearched, no chest in a garret unopened, no file of old yellow accounts to decompose in damp and worms, so keen was the hope to discover whether the boy Shakspeare poached or not, whether he held horses at the theatre door, whether he kept school, and why he left in his will only his second-best bed to Ann Hathaway, his wife.

There is somewhat touching in the madness with which the passing age mischooses the object on which all candles shine and all eyes are turned; the care with which it registers every trifle touching Queen Elizabeth and King James, and the Essexes, Leicesters, Burleighs and Buckinghams; and lets pass without a single valuable note the founder of another dynasty, which alone will cause the Tudor dynasty to be remembered,—the man who carries the Saxon race in him by the inspiration which feeds him, and on whose thoughts the foremost people of the world are now for some ages to be nourished, and minds to receive this and not another bias. A popular player;—nobody suspected he was the poet of the human race; and the secret was kept as faithfully from poets and intellectual men as from courtiers and frivolous people. (16) Bacon, who took the inventory of the human understanding for his times, never mentioned his name. Ben Jonson, though we have strained his few words of regard and panegyric, had no suspicion of the elastic fame whose first vibrations he was attempting. He no doubt thought the praise he has conceded to him generous, and esteemed himself, out of all question, the better poet of the two.

If it need wit to know wit, according to the proverb, Shakspeare's time should be capable of recognizing it. Sir Henry Wotton was born four years after Shakspeare, and died twenty-three years after him; and I find, among his correspondents and acquaintances, the following persons: Theodore Beza, Isaac Casaubon, Sir Philip Sidney, the Earl of Essex, Lord Bacon, Sir Walter Raleigh, John Milton, Sir Henry Vane, Isaac Walton, Dr. Donne, Abraham Cowley, Bellarmine, Charles Cotton, John Pym, John Hales, Kepler, Vieta, Albericus Gentilis, Paul Sarpi, Arminius; with all of whom exists some token of his having communicated, without enumerating many others whom doubtless he saw,— Shakspeare, Spenser, Jonson, Beaumont, Massinger, the two Herberts, Marlow, Chapman and the rest. Since the constellation of great men who appeared in Greece in the time of Pericles, there was never any such society;—yet their genius failed them to find out the best head in the universe. (17) Our poet's mask was impenetrable. You cannot see the mountain near. It took a century to make it suspected; and not until two centuries had passed, after his death, did any criticism which we think adequate begin to appear. It was not possible to write the history of Shakspeare till now; for he is the father of German literature: it was with the introduction of Shakspeare into German, by Lessing, and the translation of his works by Wieland and Schlegel, that the rapid burst of German literature was most intimately connected. It was not until the nineteenth century, whose speculative genius is a sort of living Hamlet, that the tragedy of Hamlet could find such wondering readers. (18) Now, literature, philosophy and thought are Shakspearized. His mind is the horizon beyond which, at present, we do not see. Our ears are educated to music by his rhythm. Coleridge and Goethe are the only critics who have expressed our convictions with any adequate fidelity: but there is in all cultivated minds a silent appreciation of his superlative power and beauty, which, like Christianity, qualifies the period.

The Shakspeare Society have inquired in all directions, advertised the missing facts, offered money for any information that will lead to proof,—and with what result? Beside some important illustration of the history of the English stage, to which I have adverted, they have gleaned a few facts touching the property, and dealings in regard to property, of the poet. It appears that from year to year he owned a larger share in the Blackfriars' Theatre: its wardrobe and other appurtenances were his: that he bought an estate in his native village with his earnings as writer and shareholder; that he lived in the best house in Stratford; was intrusted by his neighbors with their commissions in London, as of borrowing money, and the like; that he was a veritable farmer. About the time when he was writing Macbeth, he sues Philip Rogers, in the borough-court of Stratford, for thirty-five shillings, ten pence, for corn delivered to him at different times; and in all respects appears as a good husband, with no reputation for eccentricity or excess. He was a good-natured sort of man, an actor and shareholder in the theatre, not in any striking manner distinguished from other actors and managers. (19) I admit the importance of this information. It was well worth the pains that have been taken to procure it.

But whatever scraps of information concerning his condition these researches may have rescued, they can shed no light upon that infinite invention which is the concealed magnet of his attraction for us. We are very clumsy writers of history. We tell the chronicle of parentage, birth, birth-place, schooling, school-mates, earning of money, marriage, publication of books, celebrity, death; and when we have come to an end of this gossip, no ray of relation appears between it and the goddess-born; and it seems as if, had we dipped at random into the "Modern Plutarch," and read any other life there, it would have fitted the poems as well. (20) It is the essence of poetry to spring, like the rainbow daughter of Wonder, from the invisible, to abolish the past and refuse all history. Malone, Warburton, Dyce and Collier have wasted their oil. The famed theatres, Covent Garden, Drury Lane, the Park and Tremont have vainly assisted. Betterton, Garrick, Kemble, Kean and Macready dedicate their lives to this genius; him they crown, elucidate, obey and express. The genius knows them not. The recitation begins; one golden word leaps out immortal from all this painted pedantry and sweetly torments us with invitations to its own inaccessible homes. I remember I went once to see the Hamlet of a famed performer, the pride of the English stage; and all I then heard and all I now remember of the tragedian was that in which the tragedian had no part; simply Hamlet's question to the ghost:—

"What may this mean,
That thou, dead corse, again in complete steel
Revisit'st thus the glimpses of the moon?"

That imagination which dilates the closet he writes in to the world's dimension, crowds it with agents in rank and order, as quickly reduces the big reality to be the glimpses of the moon. (21) These tricks of his magic spoil for us the illusions of the green-room. Can any biography shed light on the localities into which the Midsummer Night's Dream admits me? Did Shakspeare confide to any notary or parish recorder, sacristan, or surrogate in Stratford, the genesis of that delicate creation? The forest of Arden, the nimble air of Scone Castle, the moonlight of Portia's villa, "the antres vast and desarts idle" of Othello's captivity,—where is the third cousin, or grand-nephew, the chancellor's file of accounts, or private letter, that has kept one word of those transcendent secrets? In fine, in this drama, as in all great works of art,—in the Cyclopæan architecture of Egypt and India, in the Phidian sculpture, the Gothic minsters, the Italian painting, the Ballads of Spain and Scotland,—the Genius draws up the ladder after him, when the creative age goes up to heaven, and gives way to a new age, which sees the works and asks in vain for a history.

Shakspeare is the only biographer of Shakspeare; and even he can tell nothing, except to the Shakspeare in us, that is, to our most apprehensive and sympathetic hour. (22) He cannot step from off his tripod and give us anecdotes of his inspirations. Read the antique documents extricated, analyzed and compared by the assiduous Dyce and Collier, and now read one of these skyey sentences,—aerolites,—which seem to have fallen out of heaven, and which not your experience but the man within the breast has accepted as words of fate, and tell me if they match; if the former account in any manner for the latter; or which gives the most historical insight into the man.

Hence, though our external history is so meagre, yet, with Shakspeare for biographer, instead of Aubrey and Rowe, we have really the information which is material; that which describes character and fortune, that which, if we were about to meet the man and deal with him, would most import us to know. We have his recorded convictions on those questions which knock for answer at every heart,—on life and death, on love, on wealth and poverty, on the prizes of life and the ways whereby we come at them; on the characters of men, and the influences, occult and open, which affect their fortunes; and on those mysterious and demoniacal powers which defy our science and which yet interweave their malice and their gift in our brightest hours. Who ever read the volume of the Sonnets without finding that the poet had there revealed, under masks that are no masks to the intelligent, the lore of friendship and of love; the confusion of sentiments in the most susceptible, and, at the same time, the most intellectual of men? What trait of his private mind has he hidden in his dramas? One can discern, in his ample pictures of the gentleman and the king, what forms and humanities pleased him; his delight in troops of friends, in large hospitality, in cheerful giving. Let Timon, let Warwick, let Antonio the merchant answer for his great heart. So far from Shakspeare's being the least known, he is the one person, in all modern history, known to us. What point of morals, of manners, of economy, of philosophy, of religion, of taste, of the conduct of life, has he not settled? What mystery has he not signified his knowledge of? What office, or function, or district of man's work, has he not remembered? What king has he not taught state, as Talma taught Napoleon? What maiden has not found him finer than her delicacy? What lover has he not outloved? What sage has he not outseen? What gentleman has he not instructed in the rudeness of his behavior?

Some able and appreciating critics think no criticism on Shakspeare valuable that does not rest purely on the dramatic merit; that he is falsely judged as poet and philosopher. I think as highly as these critics of his dramatic merit, but still think it secondary. He was a full man, who liked to talk; a brain exhaling thoughts and images, which, seeking vent, found the drama next at hand. (23) Had he been less, we should have had to consider how well he filled his place, how good a dramatist he was,—and he is the best in the world. But it turns out that what he has to say is of that weight as to withdraw some attention from the vehicle; and he is like some saint whose history is to be rendered into all languages, into verse and prose, into songs and pictures, and cut up into proverbs; so that the occasion which gave the saint's meaning the form of a conversation, or of a prayer, or of a code of laws, is immaterial compared with the universality of its application. So it fares with the wise Shakspeare and his book of life. He wrote the airs for all our modern music: he wrote the text of modern life; the text of manners: he drew the man of England and Europe; the father of the man in America; (24) he drew the man, and described the day, and what is done in it: he read the hearts of men and women, their probity, and their second thought and wiles; the wiles of innocence, and the transitions by which virtues and vices slide into their contraries: he could divide the mother's part from the father's part in the face of the child, or draw the fine demarcations of freedom and of fate: he knew the laws of repression which make the police of nature: and all the sweets and all the terrors of human lot lay in his mind as truly but as softly as the landscape lies on the eye. And the importance of this wisdom of life sinks the form, as of Drama or Epic, out of notice. 'T is like making a question concerning the paper on which a king's message is written.

Shakspeare is as much out of the category of eminent authors, as he is out of the crowd. He is inconceivably wise; the others, conceivably. A good reader can, in a sort, nestle into Plato's brain and think from thence; but not into Shakspeare's. We are still out of doors. For executive faculty, for creation, Shakspeare is unique. No man can imagine it better. He was the farthest reach of subtlety compatible with an individual self,—the subtlest of authors, and only just within the possibility of authorship. (25) With this wisdom of life is the equal endowment of imaginative and of lyric power. He clothed the creatures of his legend with form and sentiments as if they were people who had lived under his roof; and few real men have left such distinct characters as these fictions. And they spoke in language as sweet as it was fit. Yet his talents never seduced him into an ostentation, nor did he harp on one string. An omnipresent humanity co-ordinates all his faculties. Give a man of talents a story to tell, and his partiality will presently appear. He has certain observations, opinions, topics, which have some accidental prominence, and which he disposes all to exhibit. He crams this part and starves that other part, consulting not the fitness of the thing, but his fitness and strength. But Shakspeare has no peculiarity, no importunate topic; but all is duly given; no veins, no curiosities; no cow-painter, no bird-fancier, no mannerist is he: he has no discoverable egotism: the great he tells greatly; the small subordinately. He is wise without emphasis or assertion; he is strong, as nature is strong, who lifts the land into mountain slopes without effort and by the same rule as she floats a bubble in the air, and likes as well to do the one as the other. This makes that equality of power in farce, tragedy, narrative, and love-songs; a merit so incessant that each reader is incredulous of the perception of other readers.

This power of expression, or of transferring the inmost truth of things into music and verse, makes him the type of the poet and has added a new problem to metaphysics. This is that which throws him into natural history, as a main production of the globe, and as announcing new eras and ameliorations. Things were mirrored in his poetry without loss or blur: he could paint the fine with precision, the great with compass, the tragic and the comic indifferently and without any distortion or favor. He carried his powerful execution into minute details, to a hair point; finishes an eyelash or a dimple as firmly as he draws a mountain; and yet these, like nature's, will bear the scrutiny of the solar microscope.

In short, he is the chief example to prove that more or less of production, more or fewer pictures, is a thing indifferent. He had the power to make one picture. Daguerre learned how to let one flower etch its image on his plate of iodine, and then proceeds at leisure to etch a million. There are always objects; but there was never representation. Here is perfect representation, at last; and now let the world of figures sit for their portraits. No recipe can be given for the making of a Shakspeare; but the possibility of the translation of things into song is demonstrated.

His lyric power lies in the genius of the piece. The sonnets, though their excellence is lost in the splendor of the dramas, are as inimitable as they; and it is not a merit of lines, but a total merit of the piece; like the tone of voice of some incomparable person, so is this a speech of poetic beings, and any clause as unproducible now as a whole poem.

Though the speeches in the plays, and single lines, have a beauty which tempts the ear to pause on them for their euphuism, yet the sentence is so loaded with meaning and so linked with its foregoers and followers, that the logician is satisfied. His means are as admirable as his ends; every subordinate invention, by which he helps himself to connect some irreconcilable opposites, is a poem too. He is not reduced to dismount and walk because his horses are running off with him in some distant direction: he always rides.
The finest poetry was first experience; but the thought has suffered a transformation since it was an experience. Cultivated men often attain a good degree of skill in writing verses; but it is easy to read, through their poems, their personal history: any one acquainted with the parties can name every figure; this is Andrew and that is Rachel. The sense thus remains prosaic. It is a caterpillar with wings, and not yet a butterfly. In the poet's mind the fact has gone quite over into the new element of thought, and has lost all that is exuvial. This generosity abides with Shakespeare. We say, from the truth and closeness of his pictures, that he knows the lesson by heart. Yet there is not a trace of egotism.

One more royal trait properly belongs to the poet. I mean his cheerfulness, without which no man can be a poet,—for beauty is his aim. He loves virtue, not for its obligation but for its grace: he delights in the world, in man, in woman, for the lovely light that sparkles from them. Beauty, the spirit of joy and hilarity, he sheds over the universe. Epicurus relates that poetry hath such charms that a lover might forsake his mistress to partake of them. And the true bards have been noted for their firm and cheerful temper. Homer lies in sunshine; Chaucer is glad and erect; and Saadi says, "It was rumored abroad that I was penitent; but what had I to do with repentance?" (26) Not less sovereign and cheerful,—much more sovereign and cheerful, is the tone of Shakespeare. His name suggests joy and emancipation to the heart of men. If he should appear in any company of human souls, who would not march in his troop? He touches nothing that does not borrow health and longevity from his festal style.

And now, how stands the account of man with this bard and benefactor, when, in solitude, shutting our ears to the reverberations of his fame, we seek to strike the balance? Solitude has austere lessons; it can teach us to spare both heroes and poets; and it weighs Shakespeare also, and finds him to share the halfness and imperfection of humanity.

Shakespeare, Homer, Dante, Chaucer, saw the splendor of meaning that plays over the visible world; knew that a tree had another use than for apples, and corn another than for meal, and the ball of the earth, than for tillage and roads: that these things bore a second and finer harvest to the mind, being emblems of its thoughts, and conveying in all their natural history a certain mute commentary on human life. (27) Shakespeare employed them as colors to compose his picture. He rested in their beauty; and never took the step which seemed inevitable to such genius, namely to explore the virtue which resides in these symbols and imparts this power:—what is that which they themselves say? He converted the elements which waited on his command, into entertainments. He was master of the revels to mankind. Is it not as if one should have, through majestic powers of science, the comets given into his hand, or the planets and their moons, and should draw them from their orbits to glare with the municipal fireworks on a holiday night, and advertise in all towns, "Very superior pyrotechny this evening"? Are the agents of nature, and the power to understand them, worth no more than a street serenade, or the breath of a cigar? One remembers again the trumpet-text in the Koran,—"The heavens and the earth and all that is between them, think ye we have created them in jest?" As long as the question is of talent and mental power, the world of men has not his equal to show. But when the question is, to life and its materials and its auxiliaries, how does he profit me? What does it signify? It is but a Twelfth Night, or Midsummer-Night's Dream, or Winter Evening's Tale: what signifies another picture more or less? The Egyptian verdict of the Shakespeare Societies comes to mind; that he was a jovial actor and manager. I can not marry this fact to his verse. Other admirable men have led lives in some sort of keeping with their thought; but this man, in wide contrast. Had he been less, had he reached only the common measure of great authors, of Bacon, Milton, Tasso, Cervantes, we might leave the fact in the twilight of human fate: but that this man of men, he who gave to the science of mind a new and larger subject than had ever existed, and planted the standard of humanity some furlongs forward into Chaos,—that he should not be wise for himself;—it must even go into the world's history that the best poet led an obscure and profane life, using his genius for the public amusement. (28)

Well, other men, priest and prophet, Israelite, German and Swede, beheld the same objects: they also saw through them that which was contained. And to what purpose? The beauty straightway vanished; they read commandments, all-excluding mountainous duty; an obligation, a sadness, as of piled mountains, fell on them, and life became ghastly, joyless, a pilgrim's progress, a probation, beleaguered round with doleful histories of Adam's fall and curse behind us; with doomsdays and purgatorial and penal fires before us; and the heart of the seer and the heart of the listener sank in them.

It must be conceded that these are half-views of half-men. The world still wants its poet-priest, a reconciler, who shall not trifle, with Shakespeare the player, nor shall grope in graves, with Swedenborg the mourner; but who shall see, speak, and act, with equal inspiration. For knowledge will brighten the sunshine; right is more beautiful than private affection; and love is compatible with universal wisdom. (29)

Footnotes

Note 1.

This essay was read as a lecture in Exeter Hall, in London, in June, 1848.

Perhaps it is well to bear in mind that Mr. Emerson was reared for the ministry and ordained a clergyman, and that his ancestors for several generations had exercised that office, and moreover that, in New England, up to his day, theatrical representations had been looked at with disfavor by serious and God-fearing people, and the witnessing of such by a minister would, like dancing, have been considered unbecoming indulgence. Although Mr. Emerson emancipated himself from bonds that were merely professional or artificial, he had an inbred distaste for the common amusements of society, feeling that they were unbecoming to a scholar, and that he was not adapted for them, though he was tolerant of them in other people. There was a natural earnestness, and a simple and cheerful asceticism in his early and later life. Yet once in his later life, when he had been induced to go to see Mr. and Mrs. Barney Williams in some bright comedy, he praised their acting and admitted to his daughter that he really much enjoyed theatrical performances, in spite of the feeling that they were not for him. Dancing, for instance, which he considered a proper part of youths' education, would have seemed unbecoming for himself. He says, "It shall be writ in my memoirs ... as it was writ of St. Pachonius, Pes ejus ad saltandum non est commotus omni vita sua." His staying away from theatrical entertainments was instinctive, but he was liberal in the matter and would go to see a real artist. He even went to see the performance of the beautiful dancer Fanny Elssler, although a story which has been too often repeated of his remarks to Margaret Fuller on the subject is as false as it is silly.

In Paris he saw Rachel during the Revolution of 1848, and often told his children of her fierce and splendid declamation of the Marseillaise in the theatre, holding the tricolor aloft. On London in that same year he wrote of seeing Macready in Lear, with Mrs. Butler as Cordelia. It was to see one of Shakspeare's heroes rendered by some master that he went, and probably he never was inside a theatre twenty times in his life, and, so sensitive was he to had taste or ranting, that he was usually sorry that had gone.

The rendering of Richard II. (I cannot remember by whom) more than satisfied him, and he liked to recall the actor's tones in reading this play, an especial favorite of his, to his children. Coriolanus and Julius Cæsar too he enjoyed reading to them, and he selected passages from Shakspeare for them and trained them very carefully for their recitation in school.

He saw Edwin Booth in Boston, and met him later at the house of a friend and had some talk with him. Booth later mentioned with pleasure to their host the fact that Mr. Emerson had not once alluded to his profession or performance in their conversation.

Mr. Emerson once defined the cultivated man as "one who can tell you something new and true about Shakspeare." And he read a good omen for our age in Shakspeare's acceptance: "The book only characterizes the reader. Is Shakspeare the delight of the nineteenth century? That fact only shows whereabouts we are in the ecliptic of the soul."

In writing of Great Men in 1838 in his journal, he says:—

"Swedenborg is scarce yet appreciable. Shakspeare has, for the first time, in our time found adequate criticism, if indeed he have yet found it:—Coleridge, Lamb, Schlegel, Goethe, Very, Herder.

"The great facts of history are four or five names, Homer—Phidias—Jesus—Shakspeare. One or two names more I will not add, but see what these names stand for. All civil history and all philosophy consists of endeavours more or less vain to explain these persons."

In the journal for 1843 he writes: "Plato is weak inasmuch as he is literary. Shakspeare is not literary, but the strong earth itself." Yet from another point of view he writes, "Shakspeare and Plato each sufficed for the culture of a nation."

That Shakspeare and Milton should have been born meant much to him and to mankind. "Who saw Milton, who saw Shakspeare, saw them do their best, and utter their whole heart manlike among their contemporaries."

And again, "No man can be named whose mind still acts on the cultivated intellect of England and America with an energy comparable to that of Milton. As a poet, Shakspeare undoubtedly transcends and far surpasses him in his popularity with foreign nations: but Shakspeare is a voice merely: who and what he was that sang, that sings, we know not."

Note 2.

Mr. Emerson said of Nature:—

No ray is dimmed, no atom worn,
My oldest force is good as new,
And the fresh rose on yonder thorn
Gives back the bending heavens in dew;—

and her cheerful lesson for the artist or poet was that he too could forever re-combine the old material into fresh and splendid pictures. He rejoiced that "the poet is permitted to dip his brush into the old paint-pot with which birds, flowers, the human cheek, the living rock, the broad landscape, the ocean and the eternal sky were painted," and turning from the reading of the plays he says: "'T is Shakspeare's fault that the world appears so empty. He has educated you with his painted world, and this real one seems a huckster's-shop." Again as to his true rendering of men's characters, "I value Shakspeare as a metaphysician and admire the unspoken logic which upholds the structure of Iago, Macbeth, Antony and the rest."

Note 3.

Again the ancient doctrine of the Flowing, and the modern onward and upward stream of Evolution.

Note 4.

The passive Master lent his hand
To the vast soul that o'er him planned.
"The Problem," Poems.

Note 5.

The stage was to Shakspeare his opportunity, as the Lyceum was to Emerson.

Note 6.

Henry VIII., Act V., Scene iv.

Note 7.

This estimate of the value of memory to the poet, typified by the Greeks in their making the Muses the daughters of Mnemosyne, is enlarged upon in the Essay on "Memory" in Natural History of Intellect. Mr. Emerson said once, "Of the most romantic fact the memory is more romantic," and he quotes Quintilian as saying, Quantum ingenii, tantum memoriæ.

Note 8.

In a fragment of verse written in Mr. Emerson's journal of 1831 on the yearning of the poet to enrich himself from the Treasury of the Universe, he says:—

*And if to me it is not given
To fetch one ingot thence
Of that unfading gold of Heaven
His merchants may dispense,
Yet well I know the royal mine,*

*And know the sparkle of its ore,
Know Heaven's truth from lies that shine,—*

*Explored, they teach us to explore.
"Fragments on the Poet," Poems, Appendix.*

Note 9.

Milton, "Il Penseroso."

Note 10.

Taine, in his History of English Literature, thus justifies Chaucer's borrowing or rendering:—

"Chaucer was capable of seeking out, in the old common forest of the middle ages, stories and legends, to replant them in his own soil and make them send out new shoots…. He has the right and power of copying and translating because by dint of retouching he impresses … his original mark. He re-creates what he imitates…. At the distance of a century and a half he has affinity with the poets of Elizabeth by his gallery of pictures."

The dates of Lydgate and Caxton show a mistake as to his use of them. Caxton, following Chaucer, when he introduced the printing-press to England, printed his poems and those of Lydgate, who was younger than Chaucer. In his House of Fame, Chaucer places, in his vision, "on a pillar higher than the rest, Homer and Livy, Dares the Phrygian, Guido Colonna, Geoffrey of Monmouth and the other historians of the war of Troy" [Taine's History of English Literature], a due recognition of his debt for Troylus and Cryseyde. As for Gower, he was Chaucer's exact contemporary and friend, and Chaucer dedicated this poem to him.

Note 11.

Kipling irreverently tells of Homer's borrowings thus:—

"When 'Omer smote 'is bloomin' lyre,
He 'd 'eard men sing by land an' sea;
An' what he thought 'e might require,
'E went an' took—the same as me!"
And says of his humble audience:—

"They knew 'e stole; 'e knew they knowed.
They did n't tell, nor make a fuss,
But winked at 'Omer down the road,
An' 'e winked back—the same as us!"

Note 12.

Dr. Holmes's remark with regard to the preceding page is: "The reason why Emerson has so much to say on this subject of borrowing, especially when treating of Plato and Shakspeare, is obvious enough. He was arguing his own cause—not defending himself," etc. In Letters and Social Aims, Mr. Emerson discusses Quotation and Originality.

Note 13.

Mr. Emerson had tender associations with the Book of Common Prayer. His mother had been brought up in the Episcopal communion, and the prayer-book of her youth was always by her, though after her marriage she attended her husband's church. [In Mr. Cabot's Memoir, vol. ii. p. 572, see Mr. Emerson's letter on his mother's death.]

Note 14.

Landor says of these borrowings of Shakspeare, "He breathed upon dead bodies and brought them to life."

Note 15.

The princes Ferrex and Porrex, brothers and rivals for the ancient British throne, are characters in the tragedy Gorboduc by Norton and Sackville, to which the date 1561 is assigned. Gammer Gurton's Needle is a comedy of the same period.

Note 16.

Journal, 1864. "Shakspeare puts us all out. No theory will account for him. He neglected his works, perchance he did not know their value? Ay, but he did; witness the sonnets. He went into company as a listener, hiding himself, [Greek]; was only remembered by all as a delightful companion."

Note 17.

England's genius filled all measure
Of heart and soul, of strength and pleasure,
Gave to the mind its emperor,

And life was larger than before:
Nor sequent centuries could hit
Orbit and sum of Shakspeare's wit.
The men who lived with him became
Poets, for the air was fame.
"The Solution," Poems.

Note 18.

While writing this, Mr. Emerson was surrounded by persons paralyzed for active life in the common world by the doubts of conscience or entangled in over-fine-spun webs of their intellect. [back]

Note 19.

Journal, 1837. "I either read or inferred to-day in the Westminster Review that Shakspeare was not a popular man in his day. How true and wise. He sat alone and walked alone, a visionary poet, and came with his piece, modest but discerning, to the players, and was too glad to get it received, whilst he was too superior not to see its transcendent claims."

Note 20.

The following is the "Exordium of a lecture on Poetry and Eloquence," given in London in 1848:

"Shakspeare is nothing but a large utterance. We cannot find that anything in his age was more worth telling than anything in ours; nor give any account of his existence, but only the fact that there was a wonderful symbolizer and expresser, who has no rival in the ages, and who has thrown an accidental lustre over his time and subject."

In the lecture on "Works and Days" he wrote, "Shakspeare made his Hamlet as a bird weaves its nest." And in that on "Inspiration" in Letters and Social Aims: "Shakspeare seems to you miraculous, but the wonderful juxtapositions, parallelisms, transfers, which his genius effected, were all to him locked together as links of a chain, and the mode precisely as conceivable and familiar to higher intelligence as the index-making of the literary hack."

Journal, 1838. "Read Lear yesterday and Hamlet to-day with new wonder and mused much on the great Soul in the broad continuous daylight of these poems. Especially I wonder at the perfect reception this wit and immense knowledge of life and intellectual superiority find in us all in connection with our utter incapacity to produce anything like it. The superior tone of Hamlet in all the conversations how perfectly preserved, without any mediocrity, much less any dulness in the other speakers.

"How real the loftiness! an inborn gentleman; and above that, an exalted intellect. What incessant growth and plenitude of thought,—pausing on itself never an instant, and each sally of wit sufficient to save the play. How true then and unerring the earnest of the dialogue, as when Hamlet talks with the Queen. How terrible his discourse! What less can be said of the perfect mastery, as by a superior being, of the conduct of the drama, as the free introduction of this capital advice to the players; the commanding good sense which never retreats except before the Godhead which inspires certain passages—the more I think of it, the more I wonder. I will think nothing impossible to man. No Parthenon, no sculpture, no picture, no architecture can be named beside this. All this is perfectly visible to me and to many,—the wonderful truth and mastery of this work, of these works,—yet for our lives could not I, or any man, or all men, produce anything comparable to one scene in Hamlet or

Lear. With all my admiration of this life-like picture, set me to producing a match for it, and I should instantly depart into mouthing rhetoric.... One other fact Shakspeare presents us; that not by books are great poets made. Somewhat—and much, he unquestionably owes to his books; but you could not find in his circumstances the history of his poems. It was made without hands in his invisible world. A mightier magic than any learning, the deep logic of cause and effect he studied: its roots were cast so deep, therefore it flung out its branches so high."

Note 21.

Mr. Edwin P. Whipple, writing in Harper's Monthly in 1882, relates how in a long drive with Mr. Emerson, after a lecture, "The conversation at last drifted to contemporary actors who assumed to personate leading characters in Shakspeare's greatest plays. Had I ever seen an actor who satisfied me when he pretended to be Hamlet or Othello, Lear or Macbeth? Yes, I had seen the elder Booth in these characters. Though not perfect, he approached nearer to perfection than any other actor I knew—

"'Ah,' said Emerson, [after] the three minutes I consumed in eulogizing Booth,... 'I see you are one of the happy mortals who are capable of being carried away by an actor of Shakspeare. Now, whenever I visit the theatre to witness the performance of one of his dramas, I am carried away by the poet. I went last Tuesday to see Macready in Hamlet. I got along very well until he came to the passage:—

"thou, dead corse, again, in complete steel,
Revisit'st thus the glimpses of the moon:"—

and then actor, theatre, all vanished in view of that solving and dissolving imagination, which could reduce this big globe and all it inherits into mere "glimpses of the moon." The play went on, but, absorbed in this one thought of the mighty master, I paid no heed to it.'

"What specially impressed me, as Emerson was speaking, was his glance at our surroundings as he slowly uttered, 'glimpses of the moon,' for here above us was the same moon which must have given birth to Shakspeare's thought.... Afterward, in his lecture on Shakspeare, Emerson made use of the thought suggested in our ride by moonlight. He said, 'That imagination which dilates the closet he writes in to the world's dimensions, crowds it with agents in rank and order, as quickly reduces the big reality to be the "glimpses of the moon."'... In the printed lecture, there is one sentence declaring the absolute insufficiency of any actor, in any theatre, to fix attention on himself while uttering Shakspeare's words, which seems to me the most exquisite statement ever made of the magical suggestiveness of Shakspeare's expression. I have often quoted it, but it will bear quotation again and again, as the best prose sentence ever written on this side of the Atlantic: 'The recitation begins; one golden word leaps out immortal from all this painted pedantry, and sweetly torments us with invitations to its own inaccessible homes.'"

Note 22.

The little Shakspeare in the maiden's heart
Makes Romeo of a ploughboy on his cart;
Opens the eye to Virtue's starlike meed
And gives persuasion to a gentle deed.
"The Enchanter," Poems, Appendix.

Note 23.

And yet perhaps there is some truth in Dr. Richard Garnett's word in his Life of Emerson:

"Emerson is incapable of contemplating Shakspeare with the eye of a dramatic critic."

Just after Mr. Emerson settled in Concord he read with great pleasure Henry Taylor's play Philip van Artevelde, then recently published. He wrote in his journal for 1835:—

"I think Taylor's poem is the best light we have ever had upon the genius of Shakspeare. We have made a miracle of Shakspeare, a haze of light instead of a guiding torch, by accepting unquestioned all the tavern stories about his want of education, and total unconsciousness. The internal evidence all the time is irresistible that he was no such person. He was a man, like this Taylor, of strong sense and of great cultivation; an excellent Latin scholar, and of extensive and select reading, so as to have formed his theories of many historical characters with as much clearness as Gibbon or Niebuhr or Goethe. He wrote for intelligent persons, and wrote with intention. He had Taylor's strong good sense, and added to it his own wonderful facility of execution which aerates and sublimes all language the moment he uses it, or more truly, animates every word."

Note 24.

Lowell, in one of his essays, calls attention to the survival in New England of the type of face of the English in Queen Elizabeth's day even more than in the mother country, and also to the old English expressions, obsolete in England, but still current on New England farms.

Note 25.

Journal, 1838. fills us with wonder the first time we approach him. We go away, and work and think, for years, and come again,—he astonishes us anew. Then, having drank deeply and saturated us with his genius, we lose sight of him for another period of years. By and by we return, and there he stands immeasurable as at first. We have grown wiser, but only that we should see him wiser than ever. He resembles a high mountain which the traveller sees in the morning, and thinks he shall quickly near it and pass it, and leave it behind. But he journeys all day till noon, till night. There still is the dim mountain close by him, having scarce altered its bearings since the morning light."

Note 26.

And yet it seemeth not to me
That the high gods love tragedy;
For Saadi sat in the sun,
And thanks was his contrition;

And yet his runes he rightly read,
And to his folk his message sped.
"Saadi," Poems.

Note 27.

This image appears in "The Apology" in the Poems.

Note 28.

The Puritan shrinking from the form in which the great poet embodied his thought or oracles or dreams still appears in the journal of 1852, yet, contrasted to the dismal seers, Shakspeare is well-nigh pardoned his levity.

"There was never anything more excellent came from a human brain than the plays of Shakspeare, bating only that they were plays. The Greek has a real advantage of them in the degree in which his dramas had a religious office. Could the priest look him in the face without blenching?"

In 1839 Mr. Emerson had written:—

"It is in the nature of things that the highest originality must be moral. The only person who can be entirely independent of this fountain of literature and equal to it, must be a prophet in his own proper person. Shakspeare, the first literary genius of the world, leans on the Bible: his poetry supposes it. If we examine this brilliant influence, Shakspeare, as it lies in our minds, we shall find it reverent, deeply indebted to the traditional morality, in short, compared with the tone of the prophets, Secondary. On the other hand, the Prophets do not imply the existence of Shakspeare or Homer,—to no books or arts,—only to dread Ideas and emotions."

Note 29.

All through his life Mr. Emerson felt increasing thankfulness for "the Spirit of joy which Shakspeare had shed over the Universe." In 1864 he wrote:—

"When I read Shakspeare, as lately, I think the criticism and study of him to be in their infancy. The wonder grows of his long obscurity:—how could you hide the only man that ever wrote from all men who delight in reading?"

And again he wrote: "Your criticism is profane. Shakspeare by Shakspeare. The poet in his interlunation is a critic,"—that is, his worst is criticised by his best performance.

Journal, 1864. "How to say it I know not, but I know that the point of praise of Shakspeare is the pure poetic power: he is the chosen closet companion, who can, at any moment, by incessant surprises, work the miracle of mythologizing every fact of the common life; as snow, or moonlight, or the level rays of sunrise lend a momentary glow to Pump and wood-pile."

And again: 1836. "It is easy to solve the problem of individual existence. Why Milton, Shakspeare, or Canova should be there is reason enough. But why the million should exist drunk with the opium of Time and Custom does not appear."

But even Shakspeare must not be idolized. The soul must rely on itself, that is, on the universal fountain of beauty, wisdom and goodness to which it is open. So thus he draws the moral:—

1838. "The indisposition of men to go back to the source and mix with Deity is the reason of degradation and decay. Education is expended in the measurement and imitation of effects in the study of Shakspeare, for example, as itself a perfect being—instead of using Shakspeare merely as an effect of which the cause is with every scholar. Thus the college becomes idolatrous—a temple full of idols. Shakspeare will never be made by the study of Shakspeare. I know not how directions for greatness can be given, yet greatness may be inspired."

Feb. 1838. "Consider too how Shakspeare and Milton are formed. They are just such men as we all are to contemporaries, and none suspected their superiority,—but after all were dead, and a generation or two besides, it is discovered that they surpass all. Each of us then take the same moral to himself."

Index of Contents

To draw no envy, Shakespeare, on thy name
Am I thus ample to thy book and fame;
While I confess thy writings to be such
As neither Man nor Muse can praise too much.
'Tis true, and all men's suffrage. But these ways
Were not the paths I meant unto thy praise;
For silliest ignorance on these may light,
Which when it sounds at best but echoes right;
Or blind affection, which doth ne'er advance

The truth, but gropes, and urges all by chance;
Or crafty malice might pretend this praise,
And think to ruin where it seemed to raise.
These are as some infamous bawd or whore
Should praise a matron. What could hurt her more?
But thou art proof against them, and indeed
Above th' ill fortune of them, or the need.
I therefore will begin: Soul of the Age!
The applause, delight, the wonder of our stage!
My Shakespeare, rise; I will not lodge thee by
Chaucer, or Spenser, or bid Beaumont lie
A little further, to make thee a room:
Thou art a monument without a tomb,
And art alive still, while thy book doth live,
And we have wits to read, and praise to give.
That I not mix thee so, my brain excuses,
I mean with great but disproportioned Muses,
For if I thought my judgement were of years,
I should commit thee surely with thy peers,
And tell how far thou didst our Lyly outshine,
Or sporting Kyd, or Marlowe's mighty line.
And though thou hadst small Latin and less Greek,
From thence to honour thee I would not seek
For names; but call forth thundering Aeschylus,
Euripides, and Sophocles to us,
Pacuvius, Accius, him of Cordova dead,
To live again, to hear thy buskin tread,
And shake a stage; or, when thy socks were on,
Leave thee alone for the comparison
Of all that insolent Greece or haughty Rome
Sent forth, or since did from their ashes come.
Triumph, my Britain, thou hast one to show
To whom all scenes of Europe homage owe.
He was not of an age, but for all time!
And all the Muses still were in their prime
When, like Apollo, he came forth to warm
Our ears, or, like a Mercury, to charm!
Nature herself was proud of his designs,
And joyed to wear the dressing of his lines!
Which were so richly spun, and woven so fit,
As, since, she will vouchsafe no other wit.
The merry Greek, tart Aristophanes,
Neat Terence, witty Plautus, now not please;
But antiquated and deserted lie,
As they were not of Nature's family.
Yet must I not give Nature all; thy art,
My gentle Shakespeare, must enjoy a part.
For though the poet's matter nature be,
His art doth give the fashion; and that he
Who casts to write a living line must sweat
(Such as thine are) and strike the second heat

Upon the Muses' anvil; turn the same,
And himself with it, that he thinks to frame,
Or for the laurel he may gain a scorn;
For a good poet's made as well as born.
And such wert thou. Look how the father's face
Lives in his issue, even so the race
Of Shakespeare's mind and manners brightly shines
In his well turned and true-filed lines:
In each of which he seems to shake a lance,
As brandished at the eyes of ignorance.
Sweet swan of Avon! what a sight it were
To see thee in our waters yet appear,
And make those flights upon the banks of Thames,
That did so take Eliza and our James!
But stay, I see thee in the hemisphere
Advanced, and made a constellation there:
Shine forth, thou Star of Poets, and with rage,
Or influence, chide or cheer the drooping stage,
Which, since thy flight from hence, hath mourned like night,
And despairs day, but for thy volume's light.

Shakespeare by Matthew Arnold

Others abide our question. Thou art free.
We ask and ask—Thou smilest and art still,
Out-topping knowledge. For the loftiest hill,
Who to the stars uncrowns his majesty,

Planting his steadfast footsteps in the sea,
Making the heaven of heavens his dwelling-place,
Spares but the cloudy border of his base
To the foil'd searching of mortality;

And thou, who didst the stars and sunbeams know,
Self-school'd, self-scann'd, self-honour'd, self-secure,
Didst tread on earth unguess'd at.—Better so!

All pains the immortal spirit must endure,
All weakness which impairs, all griefs which bow,
Find their sole speech in that victorious brow

An Epitaph On The Admirable Dramatic Poet W. Shakespeare by John Milton

What needs my Shakespeare for his honored bones
The labor of an age in piled stones?
Or that his hallowed reliques should be hid
Under a star-ypointing pyramid?

Dear son of Memory, great heir of Fame,
What need'st thou such weak witness of thy name?
Thou in our wonder and astonishment
Hast built thy self a livelong monument.
For whilst, to th' shame of slow-endeavoring art,
Thy easy numbers flow, and that each heart
Hath from the leaves of thy unvalued book
Those Delphic lines with deep impression took,
Then thou, our fancy of itself bereaving,
Dost make us marble with too much conceiving,
And so sepulchred in such pomp dost lie
That kings for such a tomb would wish to die.

Shakespeare by Henry Wadsworth Longfellow

A vision as of crowded city streets,
With human life in endless overflow;
Thunder of thoroughfares; trumpets that blow
To battle; clamor, in obscure retreats,
Of sailors landed from their anchored fleets;
Tolling of bells in turrets, and below
Voices of children, and bright flowers that throw
O'er garden-walls their intermingled sweets!
This vision comes to me when I unfold
The volume of the Poet paramount,
Whom all the Muses loved, not one alone;—
Into his hands they put the lyre of gold,
And, crowned with sacred laurel at their fount,
Placed him as Musagetes on their throne.

Elegy On Mr. William Shakespeare by William Basse

Renowned Spenser, lie a thought more nigh
To learned Chaucer, and rare Beaumont lie
A little nearer Spenser, to make room
For Shakespeare in your threefold, fourfold tomb.
To lodge all four in one bed, make a shift
Until Doomsday, for hardly will a fift
Betwixt this day and that by Fate be slain,
For whom your curtains may be drawn again.
If your precedency in death doth bar
A fourth place in your sacred sepulchre,
Under this carved marble of thine own,
Sleep, rare tragedian, Shakespeare, sleep alone;
Thy unmolested peace, unshared cave
Possess as lord, not tenant of thy grave,
That unto us and others it may be

Honour hereafter to be laid by thee.

Would that in body and spirit Shakespeare came
Visible emperor of the deeds of Time,
With Justice still the genius of his rhyme,
Giving each man his due, each passion grace,
Impartial as the rain from Heaven's face
Or sunshine from the heaven-enthroned sun.
Sweet Swan of Avon, come to us again.
Teach us to write, and writing, to be men.

Thy greatest knew thee, Mother Earth; unsoured
He knew thy sons. He probed from hell to hell
Of human passions, but of love deflowered
His wisdom was not, for he knew thee well.
Thence came the honeyed corner at his lips,
The conquering smile wherein his spirit sails
Calm as the God who the white sea-wave whips,
Yet full of speech and intershifting tales,
Close mirrors of us: thence had he the laugh
We feel is thine: broad as ten thousand beeves
At pasture! thence thy songs, that winnow chaff
From grain, bid sick Philosophy's last leaves
Whirl, if they have no response-they enforced
To fatten Earth when from her soul divorced.

Most tuneful singer, lover tenderest,
Most sad, most piteous, and most musical,
Thine is the shrine more pilgrim-worn than all
The shrines of singers; high above the rest
Thy trumpet sounds most loud, most manifest.
Yet better were it if a lonely call
Of woodland birds, a song, a madrigal,
Were all the jetsam of thy sea's unrest.

For now thy praises have become too loud
On vulgar lips, and every yelping cur
Yaps thee a paean; the whiles little men,
Not tall enough to worship in a crowd,

Spit their small wits at thee. Ah! better then
The broken shrine, the lonely worshipper.

To Shakespeare (I) by Frances Anne Kemble

If from the height of that celestial sphere
Where now thou dwell'st, spirit powerful and sweet!
Thou yet canst love the race that sojourn here,
How must thou joy, with pleasure not unmeet
For thy exalted state, to know how dear
Thy memory is held throughout the earth,
Beyond the favoured land that gave thee birth.
E'en in thy seat in Heaven, thou may'st receive
Thanks, praise, and love, and wonder ever new,
From human hearts, who in thy verse perceive
All that humanity calls good and true;
Nor dost thou for each mortal blemish grieve,
They from thy glorious works have fall'n away,
As from thy soul its outward form of clay.

To Shakespeare (II) by Frances Anne Kemble

Oft, when my lips I open to rehearse
Thy wondrous spells of wisdom and of power,
And that my voice and thy immortal verse
On listening ears and hearts I mingled pour,
I shrink dismayed—and awful doth appear
The vain presumption of my own weak deed;
Thy glorious spirit seems to mine so near,
That suddenly I tremble as I read—
Thee an invisible auditor I fear:
Oh, if it might be so, my master dear!
With what beseeching would I pray to thee,
To make me equal to my noble task,
Succour from thee, how humbly would I ask,
Thy worthiest works to utter worthily.

To Shakespeare (III) by Frances Anne Kemble

Shelter and succour such as common men
Afford the weaker partners of their fate,
Have I derived from thee—from thee, most great
And powerful genius! whose sublime control,
Still from thy grave governs each human soul,
That reads the wondrous records of thy pen.

From sordid sorrows thou hast set me free,
And turned from want's grim ways my tottering feet,
And to sad empty hours, given royally,
A labour, than all leisure far more sweet:
The daily bread, for which we humbly pray,
Thou gavest me as if I were thy child,
And still with converse noble, wise, and mild,
Charmed from despair my sinking soul away;
Shall I not bless the need, to which was given
Of all the angels in the host of heaven,
Thee, for my guardian, spirit strong and bland!
Lord of the speech of my dear native land!

Shakespeare and Milton by Walter Savage Landor

The tongue of England, that which myriads
Have spoken and will speak, were paralyz'd
Hereafter, but two mighty men stand forth
Above the flight of ages, two alone;
One crying out,
All nations spoke through me.
The other:
True; and through this trumpet burst God's word;
The fall of Angels, and the doom
First of immortal, then of mortal, Man.
Glory! be glory! not to me, to God.

A Shakespeare Memorial by Alfred Austin

Why should we lodge in marble or in bronze
Spirits more vast than earth, or sea, or sky?
Wiser the silent worshipper that cons
Their words for wisdom that will never die.
Unto the favourite of the passing hour
Erect the statue and parade the bust;
Whereon decisive Time will slowly shower
Oblivion's refuse and disdainful dust.
The Monarchs of the Mind, self-sceptred Kings,
Need no memento to transmit their name:
Throned on their thoughts and high imaginings,
They are the Lords, not sycophants of Fame.
Raise pedestals to perishable stuff:
Gods for themselves are monuments enough.

Shakespeare by Mathilde Blind

Yearning to know herself for all she was,
Her passionate clash of warring good and ill,
Her new life ever ground in Death's old mill,
With every delicate detail and en masse,—
Blind Nature strove. Lo, then it came to pass,
That Time, to work out her unconscious Will,
Once wrought the Mind which she had groped for still,
And she beheld herself as in a glass.

The world of men, unrolled before our sight,
Showed like a map, where stream and waterfall
And village-cradling vale and cloud-capped height
Stand faithfully recorded, great and small;
For Shakespeare was, and at his touch, with light
Impartial as the Sun's, revealed the All.

Shakespeare by Robert Crawford

And what think ye of Shakespeare? 'Twas not he
Of Stratford is the lord of England's lyre;
Ay, not the rustic lad, whoe'er it be,
Momentous in his doing and desire.
But little Latin and less Greek? Ah, no!
It was a teeming scholar who enwrought
The wondrous pages where the wisest go
For th' culmination of the life of thought.
No jovial actor, no mere Shakescene who
Found it so hard his dear name to indite,
The marvellous pictures of our nature drew
And limned the universe in his delight.
We do not know the man; but 'twas not Will
Whose hand is on the lyre of England still.

Shakespeare by Thomas Gent

While o'er this pageant of sublunar things
Oblivion spreads her unrelenting wings,
And sweeps adown her dark unebbing tide
Man, and his mightiest monuments of pride-
Alone, aloft, immutable, sublime,
Star-like, ensphered above the track of time,
Great SHAKSPEARE beams with undiminish'd ray.
His bright creations sacred from decay,
Like Nature's self, whose living form he drew,
Though still the same, still beautiful and new.

He came, untaught in academic bowers,
A gift to Glory from the Sylvan powers:
But what keen Sage, with all the science fraught,
By elder bards or later critics taught,
Shall count the cords of his mellifluous shell,
Span the vast fabric of his fame, and tell
By what strange arts he bade the structure rise-
On what deep site the strong foundation lies?
This, why should scholiasts labour to reveal?
We all can answer it, we all can feel,
Ten thousand sympathies, attesting, start-
For SHAKSPEARE'S Temple, is the human heart!

Lord of a throne which mortal ne'er shall share-
Despot adored! he rales and revels there.
Who but has found, where'er his track hath been,
Through life's oft shifting, multifarious scene,
Still at his side the genial Bard attend,
His loved companion, counsellor, and friend!

The Thespian Sisters nurtured in the schools
Of Greece and Rome, and long coerced by rules,
Scarce moved the inmates of their native hearth
With tiny pathos and with trivial mirth,
Till She, great muse of daring enterprise,
Delighted ENGLAND! saw her SHAKSPEARE rise!

Then, first aroused in that appointed hour,
The Tragic Muse confess'd th' inspiring power;
Sudden before the startled earth she stood,
A giant spectre, weeping tears and blood;
Guilt shrunk appall'd, Despair embraced his shroud,
And Terror shriek'd, and Pity sobb'd aloud;-
Then, first Thalia with dilated ken
And quicken'd footstep pierced the walks of men;
Then Folly blush'd, Vice fled the general hiss,
Delight met Reason with a loving kiss;
At Satire's glance Pride smooth'd his low'ring crest,
The Graces weaved the dance.-And last and best
Came Momus down in Falstaff's form to earth.
To make the world one universe of mirth!

Such Sympathies the glorious Bard endear!
Thus fair he walks in Man's diurnal sphere.
But when, upborne on bright Invention's wings.
He dares the realms of uncreated things,
Forms more divine, more dreadful, start to view,
Than ever Hades or Olympus knew.
Round the dark cauldron, terrible and fell,
The midnight Witches breathe the songs of hell;
Delighted Ariel wings his fiery way

To whirl the storm, the wheeling Orbs to stay;
Then bathes in honey-dews, and sleeps in flowers;
Meanwhile, young Oberon, girt with shadowy powers,
Pursues o'er Ocean's verge the pale cold Moon,
Or hymns her, riding in her highest noon.

Thus graced, thus glorified, shall SHAKSPEARE crave
The Sculptor's skill, the pageant of the grave?
HE needs it not-but Gratitude demands
This votive offering at his Country's hands.
Haply, e'er now, from blissful bowers on high,
From some Parnassus of the empyreal sky,
Pleased, o'er this dome the gentle Spirit bends,
Accepts the gift, and hails us as his friends-
Yet smiles, perchance, to think when envious Time
O'er Bust and Urn shall bid his ivies climb,
When Palaces and Pyramids shall fall-
HIS PAGE SHALL TRIUMPH-still surviving all-
'Till Earth itself, 'like breath upon the wind,'
Shall melt away, 'nor leave a rack behind!'

Shakespeare's Mourners by John Bannister Tabb

I saw the grave of Shakespeare in a dream,
And round about it grouped a wondrous throng,
His own majestic mourners, who belong
Forever to the Stage of Life, and seem
The rivals of reality. Supreme
Stood Hamlet, as erewhile the graves among,
Mantled in thought: and sad Ophelia sung
The same swan-dirge she chanted in the stream.
Othello, dark in destiny's eclipse,
Laid on the tomb a lily. Near him wept
Dejected Constance. Fair Cordelia's lips
Moved prayerfully the while her father slept,
And each and all, inspired of vital breath,
Kept vigil o'er the sacred spoils of death.

Shakespeare by Philip Henry Savage

Through time untimed, if truly great, a Name
Reverence compels and, that forgotten, shame.
But in the stress of living you shall scan,
Yea, touch and censure, great or small, the Man.

Shakespeare by Lucretia Maria Davidson

Shakspeare!' with all thy faults, (and few have more,)
I love thee still,' and still will con thee o'er.
Heaven, in compassion to man's erring heart,
Gave thee of virtue — then, of vice a part,
Lest we, in wonder here, should bow before thee,
Break God's commandment, worship, and adore thee:
But admiration now, and sorrow join;
His works we reverence, while we pity thine.

Shakespeare by Frederick George Scott

Unseen in the great minister dome of time,
Whose shafts are centuries, its spangled roof
The vaulted universe, our master sits,
And organ-voices like a far-off chime
Roll thro' the aisles of thought. The sunlight flits

From arch to arch, and, as he sits aloof,
Kings, heroes, priests, in concourse vast, sublime,
Glances of love and cries from battle-field,
His wizard power breathes on the living air.
Warm faces gleam and pass, child, woman, man,

In the long multitude; but he, concealed,
Our bard eludes us, vainly each face we scan,
It is not he; his features are not there;
But, being thus hid, his greatness is revealed.

Shakespeare's Kingdom by Alfred Noyes

When Shakespeare came to London
He met no shouting throngs;
He carried in his knapsack
A scroll of quiet songs.

No proud heraldic trumpet
Acclaimed him on his way;
Their court and camp have perished;
The songs live on for ay.

Nobody saw or heard them,
But, all around him there,
Spirits of light and music
Went treading the April air.

He passed like any pedlar,
Yet he had wealth untold.
The galleons of th' armada
Could not contain his gold.

The kings rode on to darkness.
In England's conquering hour,
Unseen arrived her splendour;
Unknown, her conquering power.

Shakespeare 1916 by Sir Ronald Ross

Now when the sinking Sun reeketh with blood,
And the gore-gushing vapors rent by him
Rend him and bury him: now the World is dim
As when great thunders gather for the flood,
And in the darkness men die where they stood,
And dying slay, or scatter'd limb from limb
Cease in a flash where mad-eyed cherubim
Of Death destroy them in the night and mud:
When landmarks vanish—murder is become
A glory—cowardice, conscience— and to lie,
A law—to govern, but to serve a time:—
We dying, lifting bloodied eyes and dumb,
Behold the silver star serene on high,
That is thy spirit there, O Master Mind sublime.

Song, In Imitation of Shakspeare's by James Beattie

I
Blow, blow, thou vernal gale!
Thy balm will not avail
To ease my aching breast;
Though thou the billows smooth,
Thy murmurs cannot soothe
My weary soul to rest.

II
Flow, flow, thou tuneful stream!
Infuse the easy dream
Into the peaceful soul;
But thou canst not compose
The tumult of my woes,
Though soft thy waters roll.

III
Blush, blush, ye fairest flowers!

Beauties surpassing yours
My Rosalind adorn;
Nor is the Winter's blast,
That lays your glories waste,
So killing as her scorn.

IV
Breathe, breathe, ye tender lays,
That linger down the maze
Of yonder winding grove;
O let your soft control
Bend her relenting soul
To pity and to love.

V
Fade, fade, ye flowerets fair!
Gales, fan no more the air!
Ye streams, forget to glide;
Be hush'd each vernal strain;
Since nought can soothe my pain,
Nor mitigate her pride.

In A Letter To C. P. Esq. In Imitation Of Shakspeare by William Cowper

Trust me the meed of praise, dealt thriftily
From the nice scale of judgement, honours more
Than does the lavish and o'erbearing tide
Of profuse courtesy. Not all the gems
Of India's richest soil at random spread
O'er the gay vesture of some glittering dame,
Give such alluring vantage to the person,
As the scant lustre of a few, with choice
And comely guise of ornament disposed.

Shakspeare. (An Ode For His Three-Hundredth Birthday) by Martin Farquhar Tupper

I.
Immortal! risen to thy Rest,
Immortal! throned among the Blest,
Immortal! long an heir sublime
Of realms outreaching space and time,—
How shall we dare, or hope, to raise
A fitting homage of high praise
To please thy Spirit, sphered on high
Where planets roll and comets fly?
How may not thy pure fame be marr'd
By the damp breath of earthly bard,

Presuming in his zeal too bold
To gild the bright refinèd gold?
Or how canst thou, fill'd with God's love,
And tranced among the saints above,
Endure that men should seem and be
Idolaters in praise of thee!
Forgive our love, forgive our zeal,—
We cannot guess how spirits feel;
And may our homage offered thus
Please HIM who made both thee, and us!

II.
Immortal also on this darker Earth
As in those brighter spheres,
Now will we consecrate our Shakespeare's birth,
This day three hundred years!
And so from age to age for evermore
His glory shall extend,
With men of every land the wide world o'er,
Till Time itself shall end!
For, he is our's; and well with pride and joy
England may bless her son,
The Stratford scholar and the Warwick boy
That every crown hath won!
Let others boast their wisest and their best,
To each a prize may fall;
Genius gives one apiece to all the rest,
But Shakspeare claims them all!

III.
A Homer, in majestic eloquence,
A Terence, for keen wit and stinging sense,
Brighter than Pindar in his loftiest flight,
Darker than Æschylus for deeds of night,
An Ovid, in the story-pictured page,
A Juvenal, to lash the vicious age,
Graceful as Horace and more skill'd to please,
Tender as pity-stirring Sophocles,
Free as Anacreon, as Martial neat,
Than Virgil's self more delicately sweet,—
O let those ancients bend before Thee now,
And pile their many chaplets on one brow!—
Milton was great, and of divinest song,
Spenser melodious, Chaucer rough and strong,—
The vigorous Dryden, and the classic Gray,
And awful Danté, soaring far away,
Schiller and Göethe, stirring up the strife,
And Molière, dropping laughter into life,
Burns, a full spring of nature, Hood of wit,
And Tennyson, most rare and exquisite,
To each and all belongs the laurell'd crown,

And woe to him who drags their honours down,—
Yet, Shakspeare, thou wert all these lights combined,
O manysided crystal of mankind!

IV.
The jealous Moor, the thoughtful Dane,
The witty rare fat knight,
And grand old Lear half-insane,
And fell Iago's spite,
And Romeo's love, and Tybalt's hate,
And Bolinbroke in regal state,
And he that murdered sleep,—
And ruthless Shylock's bloody bond,
And Prosper with his broken wand
Long buried fathoms deep!
Frank Juliet too,— and that soft pair
Helen and Hermia, lilies fair
As growing on one stem,
Love-crazed Ophelia, drown'd ah! drown'd,
And wanton Cleopatra, crown'd
With Egypt's diadem;
The young Miranda most admired,
Cordelia's filial heart,
Sly Beatrice with wit inspired,
And Ariel's tricksey part,
Fair Rosalind,— sweet banishèd,
And gentle Desdemona — dead!—
Ay these, all these, and crowds beside,
Heroes, jesters, courtiers, clowns,
Girls in grief, or kings in pride,
Threats and crimes, and jokes, and frowns,
Witches, fairies, ghosts, and elves,
All our fancies, all ourselves,—
O! thou hast pictured with thy pen
All phases of all hearts of men,
And in thy various page survives
The Panorama of our lives!

V.
O Paragon unthought before,
O miracle of selftaught lore,
A universe of wit and worth,
The admirable Man of earth,
There is nor thing, nor thought, nor whim,
Untouch'd and unadorn'd by him;
No theme unsung, no truth untold
Of Earth's museum, new or old:
All Nature's hidden things he saw,
Intuitive to every law;
Glancing with supernal scan
At all the knowledge spelt by man;

While, for each rule and craft of Art
He grasp'd it amply, whole and part:
Like travel-wise Ulysses well he knew
Peoples and cities, men and manners too;
With shrewd but ever charitable ken
He read, and wrote out fair, the hearts of men;
Yet, in self-knowledge vers'd, a sage outright,
His giant soul was humble in its might!
O gentle, happy, modest mind,
O genial, cheerful, frank and kind,
Not even could domestic strife
Sour the sweetness of thy life,—
But wheresoe'er thy foot might roam,
Divorced from that Xantipp'd home,
Friends ever found thee,— ay, and foes,
Cordial to these, and kind to those;
Brave, loving, patient, generous, just, and good,—
Beloved by all, our matchless Shakspeare stood!

VI.
Where are thy glorious works unknown?
Who hath not heard thy fame?
On every shore, in every zone,
The World, with glad acclaim,
Yea, from the cottage to the throne,
Hath magnified thy name!
From far Australia to Vancouver's pines,
From the High Alps to Russia's deepest mines,
From China, with her English lesson learnt,
To Chili, wailing for her daughters burnt;
There, everywhere, our Shakspeare breathes and moves
In the sweet ether of all human loves!—
Where rent America now writhes in woe,
Where Nile and Danube, Thames and Ganges flow,
Wherever England sails, and human kind
Anywhere feels in heart, and thinks in mind,
There, everywhere, our Shakspeare's voice is heard,
By him all souls are thrill'd, and cheer'd, and stirr'd;
Each passion flows or ebbs, as Shakspeare speaks,
Hate knits the brow, or terror pales the cheeks,
Love lights the eyes, or pity melts the heart,
And all men bow beneath our Poet's art!

VII.
What monument to rear,
What worthy offering?—
Nought lacks thy glory here
Of all thy sons can bring:
Long since, a twin-sphered brother spake,
How vain it were to raise
To such a Name, for Memory's sake,

Its pyramid of praise:
Our Shakspeare needs no sculptured stones,
No temple for his honoured bones!
But haply in his native street
Beside the rescued home
Hallowed by his infant feet
Whereto all pilgrims roam,
A College well might rear its head,
That Townsman's name to bear,
And brother-actors' sons he bred
To light and learning there!
And, for great London and its throngs,—
To Shakspeare of old right belongs
The Shakspeare Bridge, with Shakspeare scenes
Sculptured upon its pannell'd screens,
Colossus-like the Thames to span,
And telling every passing man
Where a poor player in his youth
Served Heaven and Earth by mimic truth,
And wrapped in Art's and Nature's robe,
Leased,— 'twas his Heritage, — the Globe!—

VIII.
Great Magician for all time,
Denizen of every clime,
Darling poet of mankind,
Master of the human mind,
Nature's very priest and king,—
Take the gifts thy children bring!
Let thy Spirit, hovering o'er
Thine earthly home and haunts of yore,
In its wisdom, wealth, and worth,
Shine upon us from above,
While thy kinsmen here on earth
Thus with pious care and love
Celebrate our Shakspeare's birth.

On The Site of A Mulberry-Tree; Planted By Wm. Shakspeare; Felled By The Rev. F. Gastrell by Dante Gabriel Rossetti

This tree, here fall'n, no common birth or death
Shared with its kind. The world's enfranchised son,
Who found the trees of Life and Knowledge one,
Here set it, frailer than his laurel-wreath.
Shall not the wretch whose hand it fell beneath
Rank also singly—the supreme unhung?
Lo! Sheppard, Turpin, pleading with black tongue
This viler thief's unsuffocated breath!
We'll search thy glossary, Shakspeare! whence almost,

And whence alone, some name shall be reveal'd
For this deaf drudge, to whom no length of ears
Sufficed to catch the music of the spheres;
Whose soul is carrion now,—too mean to yield
Some Starveling's ninth allotment of a ghost.

www.ingramcontent.com/pod-product-compliance
Lightning Source LLC
Chambersburg PA
CBHW060308050426
42448CB00009B/1767